William E. Poole's
American
Home

110

Classic Home Plans

Published by Hanley Wood
One Thomas Circle, NW, Suite 600
Washington, DC 20005

DISTRIBUTION CENTER
PBD
Hanley Wood Consumer Group
3280 Summit Ridge Parkway
Duluth, Georgia 30096

Vice President, Home Plans, Andrew Schultz
Associate Publisher, Editorial Development, Jennifer Pearce
Managing Editor, Hannah McCann
Editor, Simon Hyoun
Assistant Editor, Kimberly Johnson
Publications Manager, Brian Haefs
Production Manager, Melissa Curry
Director, Plans Marketing, Mark Wilkin
Senior Plan Merchandiser, Nicole Phipps
Plan Merchandiser, Hillary Huff
Graphic Artist, Joong Min
Plan Data Team Leader, Susan Jasmin
Marketing Director, Holly Miller
Marketing Manager, Brett Bryant

Most Hanley Wood titles are available at quantity discounts with bulk
purchases for educational, business, or sales promotional use. For information, please contact Andrew Schultz at aschultz@hanleywood.com.

BIG DESIGNS, INC.
PRESIDENT, CREATIVE DIRECTOR Anthony D'Elia
VICE PRESIDENT, BUSINESS MANAGER Megan D'Elia
VICE PRESIDENT, DESIGN DIRECTOR Chris Bonavita
EDITORIAL DIRECTOR John Roach
ASSISTANT EDITOR Carrie Atkinson
SENIOR ART DIRECTOR Stephen Reinfurt
PRODUCTION DIRECTOR David Barbella
PRODUCTION MANAGER Rich Fuentes
PHOTO EDITOR Christine DiVuolo
ART DIRECTOR Frank Augugliaro
GRAPHIC DESIGNER Billy Doremus

PHOTO CREDITS

10 9 8 7 6 5 4 3 2 1

Printed in the United States of America

Library of Congress Control Number: 2006925915

ISBN-13: 978-1-931131-64-3
ISBN-10: 1-931131-64-3

William E. Poole's
American Home

58

95

5

About The Designer

William E. Poole

Grew up in a Raleigh housing project during a time when you did not need to lock your doors. Though raised with lots of love, we were poor and I began to appreciate the significance of home ownership and all that it implies.

At age 7, convinced an acclaimed artist and professor that I had talent. She befriended me and I became the only boy attending art classes at an all-girls' college ... wow!

Received a full scholarship to North Carolina State University School of Design. Was devastated when I had to leave to help support my widowed mother and four younger siblings.

Hindsight renders all things in proper perspective. Missing the total indoctrination of the modern school of thought was not all bad. Escaped with my love for the classics. Self-taught after that and then the fun began.

Started my business, married my first love, became a pilot (one of the many seemingly impossible dreams), enjoyed photography, follow the horses, love the West, fishing and have a "zoo" at home--yet, continue to consume the classics with always an emphasis on home. Designed The Natchez, America's most popular home design, which set forth a national trend for front porches in residential architecture. Have almost one million families living in homes of my design. Created my own lines of furniture, accessories, and building products (three more of my impossible dreams).

Son John works with me and is a noted designer in his own right. Haven't gotten the notion to be put to pasture. Still a lot left to do—a lot of dreams yet to fulfill.

Enjoy a glass of
lemonade on
the expansive
front porch.

The Hudson Valley

As an everyday dwelling or a weekend retreat,
there's a home here to meet your need

A romantic getaway, a year-round haven from the daily grind-a home can be all these things and more. Like the plans found in "Romantic Cottages and Getaways," the Hudson Valley's warmth and charm is a welcome respite. Inspired by styles as far away as the West Indies and as near as the pristine Connecticut countryside, there is a look and a layout here for everyone.

The Hudson Valley is a Dutch Colonial home with all the trimmings. On the outside, the flared eaves of a side-gabled roof reveal the design's Dutch origins and provide shelter for the full-width front porch. Inside, the Colonial influence continues, with a country flare.

Romantic Cottages and Getaways

The gently flared eaves of the roof are tell-tale signs of Dutch Colonial design.

Out on the trail, exhausted by the crisp morning air and the pounding hooves beneath me, I turned my mount towards home, a warm crackling fire, and breakfast. The best place I could ever hope to be— the Hudson Valley, my Dutch Colonial home.

ABOVE: Hardwood floors complement a stone hearth centerpiece in the family room. RIGHT: A Dutch door fits right in with the home's Dutch Colonial design.

A traditional layout at the plan's entrance places the formal living room and dining room on either side of a central hallway. Like the homes in this section, a more modern layout can be found at the rear of the home, where a casual family room opens to an island kitchen. This space keeps conversation and activities flowing from room to room. This kitchen includes a convenient walk-in pantry and a front stoop: use this doorway as a "friends and family" entrance and reserve the front door for formal guests.

On the opposite side of the plan, modernity guides a luxurious master suite. This room was made to pamper the homeowners by offering a master bath with two vanity

Columns support a series of arches defining the foyer from the formal dining room.

HPK3100001

FIRST FLOOR: 3,016 SQ. FT.

SECOND FLOOR: 1,283 SQ. FT.

TOTAL: 4,299 SQ. FT.

BONUS SPACE: 757 SQ. FT.

BEDROOMS: 4

BATHROOMS: 4½ + ½

WIDTH: 105' - 0"

DEPTH: 69' - 0"

FOUNDATION: CRAWLSPACE

ORDER ONLINE @ EPLANS.COM

An island provides storage and counter space while the wood ceiling beams creatively display pots, pans, and baskets in this country kitchen.

sinks, a separate shower, a whirlpool tub, and a compartmented toilet; and a massive walk-in closet suits the most ambitious wardrobes.

Upstairs, three more bedrooms each have their own walk-in closets and private baths. Above the garage, bonus space is large enough for a recreation room and a fourth bedroom and bath. The plans within "Romantic Cottages and Getaways" are so well-suited to serve as second homes, that this space could be equally useful as a seasonal storage room. ∎

SECOND FLOOR

FIRST FLOOR

HPK3100111

First Floor: 1,201 sq. ft.

Second Floor: 708 sq. ft.

Total: 1,909 sq. ft.

Bedrooms: 3

Bathrooms: 2½

Width: 56' - 8"

Depth: 39' - 8"

Foundation: Crawlspace

ORDER ONLINE @ EPLANS.COM

SECOND FLOOR

FIRST FLOOR

Low Country Cottage

Going south towards Charleston, near the quaint old SeeWee restaurant (another story unto itself), take a left to McClellansville. This sleepy little undiscovered fishing village, with it's winding roads, rustic church, picket fences and easy way of living transports one back to the days of Tom Sawyer and Huck Finn. It is here that the Low Country Cottage lives beneath the swaying boughs and sunlit skies of both yesteryear and now.

Miles Melton

SECOND FLOOR

ROOF AREA

CEILING BREAK LINE
WARDROBE
CEILING BREAK LINE

BEDROOM 3
12'0"X13'6"

OPEN TO BELOW

STORAGE

WARDROBE
SHELV

FUTURE REC. ROOM
21'0"X17'0"

CEILING BREAK LINE

CEILING BREAK LINE

HANDRAIL

BEDROOM 2
12'0"X15'0"

STORAGE

BALCONY

LOUNGE

CEILING BREAK LINE

VANITY

BATH 2

ROOF AREA

FIRST FLOOR

SCREEN PORCH

BREAKFAST
AREA
12'0"X9'0"

VAULTED CEILING

GREAT ROOM
18'0"X17'4"

MASTER
BEDROOM
12'0"X17'0"

2 CAR GARAGE
21'0"X26'0"

BAR

KITCHEN
12'0"X12'0"

ENTERTAINMENT
CENTER

PANTRY

UTILITY

PDR
ROOM

DRY WASH

DINING ROOM
12'4"X11'0"

FOYER
5'8"X11'0"

WARDROBE

MASTER
BATH

VANITY

LIN

WHIRLPOOL
TUB

SHWR.

INTERIOR PRIVACY
SHUTTERS

© William E. Poole Designs

COVERED PORCH

HPK3100002

FIRST FLOOR: 1,370 SQ. FT.

SECOND FLOOR: 668 SQ. FT.

TOTAL: 2,038 SQ. FT.

BONUS SPACE: 421 SQ. FT.

BEDROOMS: 3

BATHROOMS: 2½

WIDTH: 71' - 8"

DEPTH: 49' - 4"

FOUNDATION: Crawlspace

ORDER ONLINE @ EPLANS.COM

Shenandoah II

The Shenandoah II is a home built for celebrations. They began the day our family moved into this wonderful home and still continue through the years. The crisp air of autumn finds a line-up of smiling jack-o'-lanterns, and soon it will be time to wind the stately columns with twinkling lights that brighten the snowy, silent nights. In a blink of an eye, the first signs of spring provide a colorful backdrop for hidden Easter eggs. And on the Fourth of July, the Stars and Stripes will proudly wave. At Shenandoah II, each day is a celebration of home and family. May the celebrations live on—here's to a wonderful life!

Port Royal

Every evening after supper, Uncle Henry wanders outdoors to the front porch. He has a ritual from which he never strays. As twilight settles in, he finishes his pipe and slowly unfolds his lanky frame from the creaky rocking chair. He is ready to rosin up his bow and strike the first lively chords of our favorite fiddle tunes. Many pleasant evenings are spent telling tales and making music at the Port Royal.

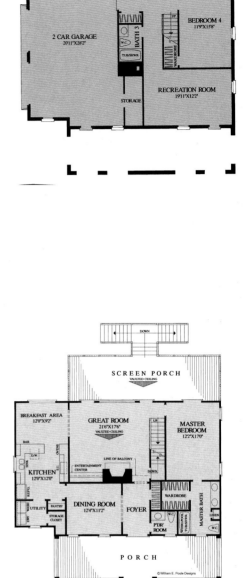

2 CAR GARAGE
20'11"X28'2"

BATH 3

W.C.

TUB/SHWR.

STORAGE

BEDROOM 4
11'9"X15'8"

WARDROBE

RECREATION ROOM
19'11"X12'2"

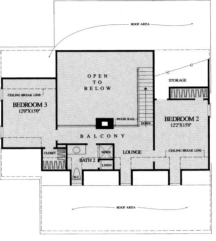

ROOF AREA

OPEN
TO
BELOW

STORAGE

CEILING BREAK LINE

BEDROOM 3
12'0"X15'0"

WOOD RAIL

DOWN

BEDROOM 2
12'2"X15'0"

BALCONY

CLOSET

LOUNGE

CEILING BREAK LINE

BATH 2

SHWR.

LINEN

W.C.

ROOF AREA

SECOND FLOOR

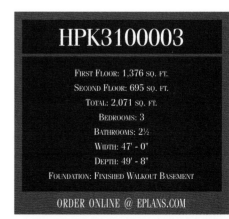

DOWN

SCREEN PORCH
VAULTED CEILING

BREAKFAST AREA
12'0"X9'2"

GREAT ROOM
21'6"X17'6"
VAULTED CEILING

UP

MASTER
BEDROOM
12'2"X17'0"

BAR

D.W.

SINK

OVENS

LINE OF BALCONY

DN.

KITCHEN
12'0"X12'0"

REFRIG.

ENTERTAINMENT
CENTER

DOWN

WARDROBE

DRY. WASH.

UTILITY

PANTRY

DINING ROOM
12'4"X11'2"

FOYER

MASTER BATH

STORAGE
CLOSET

WHIRLPOOL
TUB/SHWR.

LINEN

P'DR'
ROOM

W.C.

W.C.

© William E. Poole Designs

PORCH

FIRST FLOOR

HPK3100003

FIRST FLOOR: 1,376 SQ. FT.

SECOND FLOOR: 695 SQ. FT.

TOTAL: 2,071 SQ. FT.

BEDROOMS: 3

BATHROOMS: 2½

WIDTH: 47' - 0"

DEPTH: 49' - 8"

FOUNDATION: Finished Walkout Basement

Cape Cod Cottage

A soft breeze blowing in from the sea lightly ruffles your hair as you recall the wonderful summers you spent here as a child. Borrowing from the essence and style of Cape Cod—a place that captures the heart—your dream is now a reality. This cozy cottage you call your own is embellished with weathered blue shutters and surrounded by a white picket fence. Your Cape Cod Cottage, with its welcoming warmth, is a grand place to call "home."

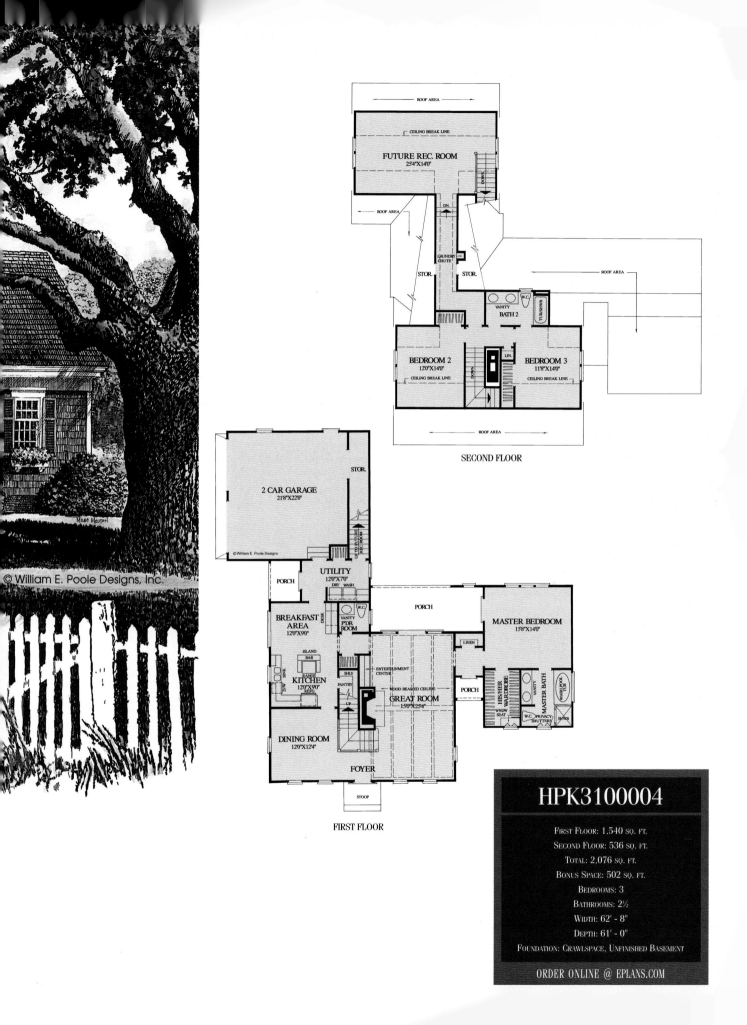

© William E. Poole Designs, Inc.

SECOND FLOOR

ROOF AREA

CEILING BREAK LINE

FUTURE REC. ROOM
25'4"X14'0"

ROOF AREA

DN

ROOF AREA

LAUNDRY CHUTE

STOR.

STOR.

W.C.

VANITY

TUB/SHWR

BATH 2

ROOF AREA

BEDROOM 2
12'0"X14'0"

LIN.

DOWN

BEDROOM 3
11'8"X14'0"

CEILING BREAK LINE

CEILING BREAK LINE

ROOF AREA

FIRST FLOOR

2 CAR GARAGE
21'8"X22'0"

STOR.

© William E. Poole Designs

UP TO FUTURE REC ROOM

PORCH

UTILITY
12'0"X7'0"

DRY   WASH

DESK

W.C.

VANITY

PDR ROOM

PORCH

MASTER BEDROOM
15'8"X14'0"

BREAKFAST AREA
12'0"X9'0"

ISLAND BAR

SINK

D/W

RANGE

KITCHEN
12'0"X9'0"

REFG.

SHLV

PANTRY

UP

ENTERTAINMENT CENTER

WOOD BEAMED CEILING

GREAT ROOM
15'0"X25'4"

LINEN

PORCH

HIS/HER WARDROBE

VANITY

MASTER BATH

WHIRLPOOL TUB

DINING ROOM
12'0"X12'4"

FOYER

WNDW SEAT

W.C.

PRIVACY SHUTTERS

SHWR

STOOP

HPK3100004

FIRST FLOOR: 1,540 SQ. FT.

SECOND FLOOR: 536 SQ. FT.

TOTAL: 2,076 SQ. FT.

BONUS SPACE: 502 SQ. FT.

BEDROOMS: 3

BATHROOMS: 2½

WIDTH: 62' - 8"

DEPTH: 61' - 0"

FOUNDATION: CRAWLSPACE, UNFINISHED BASEMENT

ORDER ONLINE @ EPLANS.COM

Fairview

They were so glad to find this house. They had searched high and low for their perfect retirement home. Everything worked so perfectly all on one level. They quickly realized, had they begun married life here and expanded the upper level as children came along, it would have remained the perfect home for them—both then and now.

ROOF AREA

CATHEDRAL CEILING   ROOF AREA

OPEN TO BELOW

9'-0" CEILING BREAKLINE

DOWN   8'-0" CEILING BREAKLINE

FUTURE BONUS
14'-0" X 22'-5"

9'-0" CEILING BREAKLINE

9'-0" CEILING BREAKLINE

DOWN

UNFINISHED STORAGE

9'-0" CEILING BREAKLINE

ROOF AREA

WARDROBE
8'-4" X 9'-0"

MASTER BEDROOM
13'-0" X 16'-0"

LIN.

TERRACE AREA

WHIRLPOOL TUB

MASTER BATH   UTILITY   SINK   PANTRY   BREAKFAST
10'-0" X 12'-0"

D.   W.   REFG.

BOOK CASE

BEDROOM 3
12'-0" X 11'-8"

GREAT ROOM
14'-0" X 18'-10"
CATHEDRAL CEILING

SINK

LINEN

2 CAR GARAGE
21'-8" X 22'-0"

RANGE

KITCHEN
12'-6" X 12'-6"

DW

BATH 2

STORAGE   UP

©William E. Poole Designs

DINING ROOM
13'-0" X 13'-0"   FOYER
5'-8" X 11'-0"   BEDROOM 2
12'-0" X 13'-0"

PORCH
35'-8" X 8'-0"

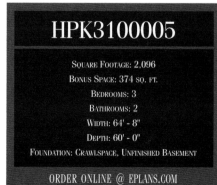

HPK3100005

Square Footage: 2,096
Bonus Space: 374 sq. ft.
Bedrooms: 3
Bathrooms: 2
Width: 64' - 8"
Depth: 60' - 0"
Foundation: Crawlspace, Unfinished Basement

ORDER ONLINE @ EPLANS.COM

HPK3100006

FIRST FLOOR: 1,588 SQ. FT.

SECOND FLOOR: 537 SQ. FT.

TOTAL: 2,125 SQ. FT.

BEDROOMS: 3

BATHROOMS: 2½

WIDTH: 30' - 8"

DEPTH: 56' - 2"

FOUNDATION: CRAWLSPACE

ORDER ONLINE @ EPLANS.COM

The Ramblewood

Inspiration comes frequently as though out-of-the-blue—sometimes like a lightening bolt, other times like a slowly evolving yet perfect sunrise. The Ramblewood is a perfectly conceived and executed cottage full of abundant individuality and charm that flows and functions with ease for the fortunate family within. The home itself exudes inspiration for love, romance, and future dreams.

SECOND FLOOR

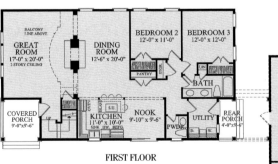

FIRST FLOOR

© William E. Poole Designs, Inc.

HPK3100007

SQUARE FOOTAGE: 2,151
BEDROOMS: 3
BATHROOMS: 2
WIDTH: 61' - 0"
DEPTH: 55' - 8"
FOUNDATION: CRAWLSPACE, UNFINISHED BASEMENT

ORDER ONLINE @ EPLANS.COM

Country Cottage

Every neighborhood has the perfect little Country Cottage just down the lane, all tucked into the perfect little yard. Simple, warmly detailed, and much loved, everyone who passes feels that (should they enter) they would be greeted with a welcoming smile. All the children in the neighborhood know that "Mother Goose" lives there because a hug, a lap, and a nursery rhyme await them (along with milk and cookies) when they visit—which is often.

Eastern Shore Cottage

Being of incisive line, thought, style, and effect, the understated appeal of the Eastern Shore Cottage is reminiscent of a simpler life. Times when neighbor greeted neighbor, doors were left unlocked, and a helping hand was near. We can have that again. Choose your neighborhood, plan your home—you've made a wise decision.

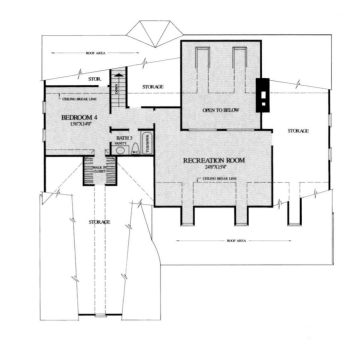

HPK3100008

SQUARE FOOTAGE: 2,151

BONUS SPACE: 814 SQ. FT.

BEDROOMS: 3

BATHROOMS: 2

WIDTH: 61' - 0"

DEPTH: 55' - 8"

FOUNDATION: CRAWLSPACE, UNFINISHED BASEMENT

ORDER ONLINE @ EPLANS.COM

© William E.

Planters Cottage

Planter's cottages were raised one-and-a-half-story homes that overlooked the rivers and captured their breezes. Though life was hard in those early times, each day began fresh amid the first rays of light and closed with the promise of another peaceful night.

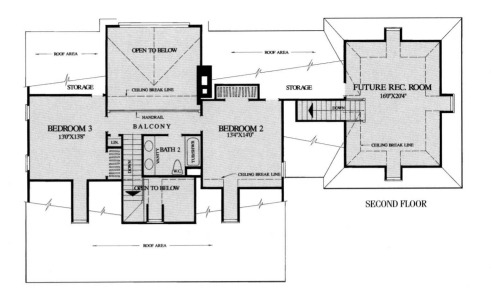

ROOF AREA

STORAGE

OPEN TO BELOW

ROOF AREA

STORAGE

FUTURE REC. ROOM
16'0"X20'4"

CEILING BREAK LINE

BEDROOM 3
13'0"X13'8"

HANDRAIL

BALCONY

LIN.

DOWN

VANITY

BATH 2

W.C.

TUB/SHWR

BEDROOM 2
13'4"X14'0"

CEILING BREAK LINE

DOWN

CEILING BREAK LINE

OPEN TO BELOW

SECOND FLOOR

ROOF AREA

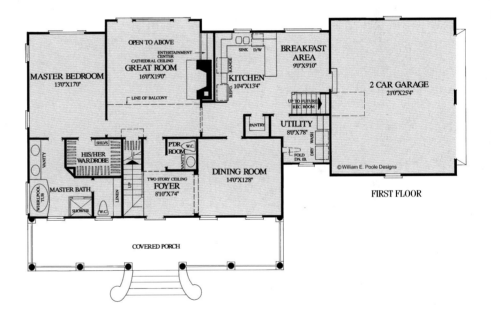

OPEN TO ABOVE

ENTERTAINMENT
CENTER

CATHEDRAL CEILING

GREAT ROOM
16'0"X19'0"

LINE OF BALCONY

RANGE

SINK

D/W

KITCHEN
10'4"X13'4"

BREAKFAST
AREA
9'0"X9'10"

2 CAR GARAGE
21'0"X25'4"

MASTER BEDROOM
13'0"X17'0"

REFRIG

PANTRY

UP TO FUTURE
REC. ROOM

UTILITY
8'0"X7'8"

WASH

DRY

VANITY

HIS/HER
WARDROBE

SHLVS

P'DR
ROOM

W.C.

FOLD
DN. IB.

©William E. Poole Designs

UP

VANITY

WHIRLPOOL
TUB

MASTER BATH

SHOWER

W.C.

LINEN

FOYER
8'10"X7'4"

TWO STORY CEILING

DINING ROOM
14'0"X12'8"

FIRST FLOOR

COVERED PORCH

HPK3100009

FIRST FLOOR: 1,556 SQ. FT.

SECOND FLOOR: 623 SQ. FT.

TOTAL: 2,179 SQ. FT.

BONUS SPACE: 368 SQ. FT.

BEDROOMS: 3

BATHROOMS: 2½

WIDTH: 73' - 4"

DEPTH: 41' - 4"

FOUNDATION: Crawlspace, Finished Basement

ORDER ONLINE @ EPLANS.COM

Chevy Chase

Administrations change. History is made. Policies are set. Technology advances. The pace is fast—the future unknown. The result: stress. Yet, solace, that elusive element in our lives, is found each day in the space of home—at Chevy Chase.

© William E. Poole Designs, Inc.

MASTER BEDROOM
13'0"X17'0"

MASTER BATH

W.C.

LAV.

WHIRLPOOL TUB

SHWR.

SEAT

LINEN

WARDROBE

STORAGE

SINK

UTILITY

WASH

DRY

STORAGE

BREAKFAST AREA
12'0"X10'0"

BAR

SINK

D.W.

KITCHEN
12'0"X12'4"

REFR.

PANTRY

OVENS

FAMILY ROOM
16'10"X20'0"

BOOKCASE

BEDROOM 2
12'4"X13'0"

LAV.

WALK IN CLOSET

BATH 2

W.C.

TUB/SHWR.

WALK IN CLOSET

2 CAR GARAGE
23'8"X24'0"

DINING ROOM
12'0"X13'0"

FOYER
8'0"X11'8"

LINEN

BEDROOM 3
12'0"X11'8"

BATH 3

LAV.

W.C.

TUB/SHWR.

P O R C H

© William E. Poole Designs

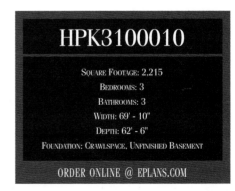

HPK3100010

SQUARE FOOTAGE: 2,215
BEDROOMS: 3
BATHROOMS: 3
WIDTH: 69' - 10"
DEPTH: 62' - 6"
FOUNDATION: CRAWLSPACE, UNFINISHED BASEMENT

ORDER ONLINE @ EPLANS.COM

Valdosta

Miss Margaret has lived here all her life—along with her brothers, sisters, cousins, and grandparents. The Valdosta has been their home forever. It is with many fond memories that she bids a final farewell to the Valdosta and wishes happiness and joy for the new family ready to begin their sojourn within.

liam E. Poole Designs, Inc.

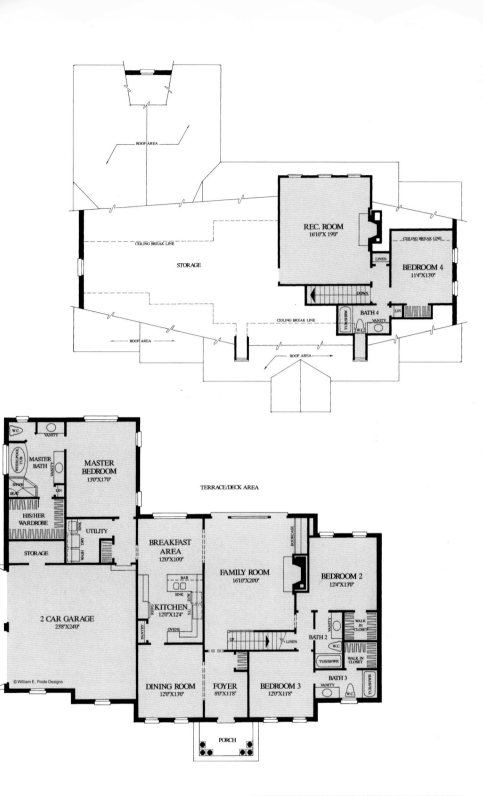

ROOF AREA

REC. ROOM
16'10"X 19'0"

CEILING BREAK LINE

STORAGE

CEILING BREAK LINE

LINEN

BEDROOM 4
11'4"X13'0"

DOWN

CEILING BREAK LINE

TUB/SHWR

BATH 4

LIN

W.C.

VANITY

ROOF AREA

ROOF AREA

W.C.

VANITY

WHIRLPOOL TUB

MASTER BATH

MASTER BEDROOM
13'0"X17'0"

TERRACE/DECK AREA

SHWR

SEAT

LIN

HIS/HER WARDROBE

STORAGE

SINK

UTILITY

WASH

DRY

BREAKFAST AREA
12'0"X10'0"

BOOKCASE

FAMILY ROOM
16'10"X20'0"

BEDROOM 2
12'4"X13'0"

2 CAR GARAGE
23'8"X24'0"

PANTRY

REFRG

KITCHEN
12'0"X12'4"

BAR

SINK

D/W

OVENS

UP

LINEN

BATH 2

VANITY

WALK IN CLOSET

W.C.

TUB/SHWR

WALK IN CLOSET

© William E. Poole Designs

DINING ROOM
12'0"X13'0"

FOYER
8'0"X11'8"

BEDROOM 3
12'0"X11'8"

BATH 3

VANITY

W.C.

TUB/SHWR

PORCH

HPK3100011

SQUARE FOOTAGE: 2,215
BEDROOMS: 3
BATHROOMS: 3
WIDTH: 69' - 10"
DEPTH: 60' - 6"
FOUNDATION: CRAWLSPACE, UNFINISHED BASEMENT

ORDER ONLINE @ EPLANS.COM

MILES MELTON

Turnberry

Aunt Harriet lived in a home much like the Turnberry. She wore wide-brimmed, flowered hats and never went calling without first donning her white cotton gloves. But every day of her life was an adventure. While watching a well-known comedy, my cousin B.J. and I, between fits of laughter, agreed the leading lady fit Aunt Harriet, right down to her familiar white gloves. As time marches on, this home's unique character will continue on and on—delightful, timeless. Like Aunt Harriet.

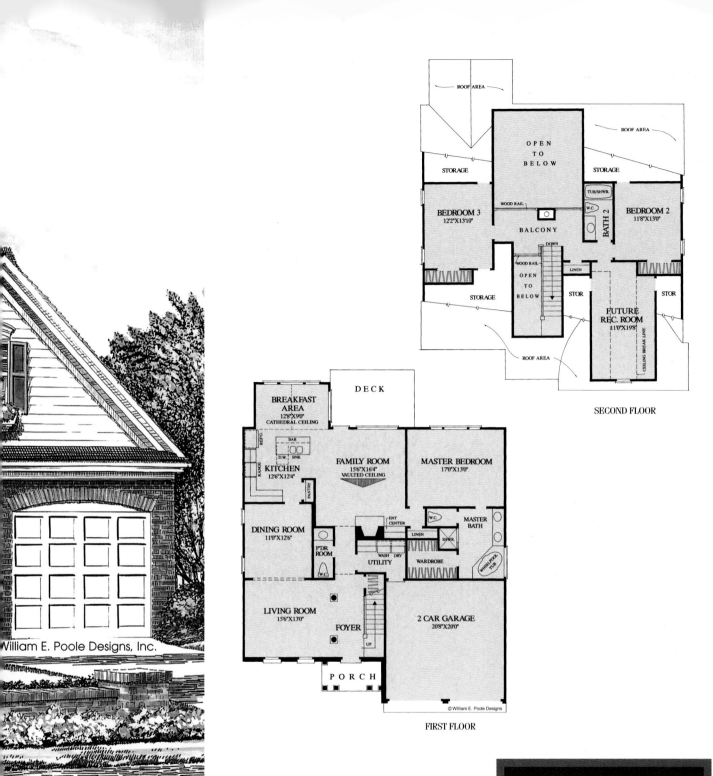

William E. Poole Designs, Inc.

SECOND FLOOR

ROOF AREA

ROOF AREA

OPEN TO BELOW

STORAGE

STORAGE

WOOD RAIL

BEDROOM 3
12'2"X13'10"

TUB/SHWR.

W.C.

BATH 2

BEDROOM 2
11'8"X13'0"

BALCONY

WOOD RAIL

OPEN TO BELOW

DOWN

LINEN

STORAGE

STOR

STOR

FUTURE REC. ROOM
11'0"X19'8"

CEILING BREAK LINE

ROOF AREA

FIRST FLOOR

DECK

BREAKFAST AREA
12'8"X9'0"
CATHEDRAL CEILING

REFG.

BAR

D.W. SINK

KITCHEN
12'6"X12'4"

RANGE

FAMILY ROOM
15'6"X16'4"
VAULTED CEILING

MASTER BEDROOM
17'0"X13'0"

PANTRY

DINING ROOM
11'0"X12'6"

ENT CENTER

W.C.

MASTER BATH

P'DR ROOM

LINEN

SHWR

W.C.

WASH DRY

UTILITY

WARDROBE

WHIRLPOOL TUB

LIVING ROOM
15'6"X13'0"

FOYER

UP

2 CAR GARAGE
20'8"X20'0"

PORCH

©William E. Poole Designs

HPK3100012

FIRST FLOOR: 1,634 SQ. FT.

SECOND FLOOR: 619 SQ. FT.

TOTAL: 2,253 SQ. FT.

BONUS SPACE: 229 SQ. FT.

BEDROOMS: 3

BATHROOMS: 2½

WIDTH: 46' - 0"

DEPTH: 54' - 5"

FOUNDATION: CRAWLSPACE, SLAB

ORDER ONLINE @ EPLANS.COM

HPK3100013

SQUARE FOOTAGE: 2,256

BONUS SPACE: 862 SQ. FT.

BEDROOMS: 3

BATHROOMS: 2½

WIDTH: 61' - 4"

DEPTH: 66' - 8"

FOUNDATION: Crawlspace, Unfinished Basement

ORDER ONLINE @ EPLANS.COM

Seabrook Cottage

As the plane taxied down the runway, the anticipation within was palpable. They were met by the breeder who took them on a winding journey down dusty, rural back roads to her home. There, nestled in a small cove, was the picturesque "Seabrook Cottage." It was perfect. And—inside were the two beautiful little Devon Rex kittens who were flying home with them to complete their family. What a joyful day!

SECOND FLOOR

FIRST FLOOR

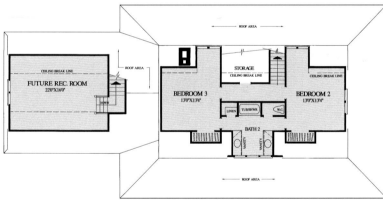

ROOF AREA

CEILING BREAK LINE

FUTURE REC. ROOM
22'0"X16'0"

ROOF AREA

DOWN

STORAGE
CEILING BREAK LINE

BEDROOM 3
13'0"X13'4"

BEDROOM 2
13'0"X13'4"

CEILING BREAK LINE

LINEN | TUB/SHWR | W.C.

BATH 2

VANITY | VANITY

ROOF AREA

SECOND FLOOR

HPK3100014

FIRST FLOOR: 1,601 SQ. FT.

SECOND FLOOR: 667 SQ. FT.

TOTAL: 2,268 SQ. FT.

BONUS SPACE: 378 SQ. FT.

BEDROOMS: 3

BATHROOMS: 2½

WIDTH: 83' - 4"

DEPTH: 39' - 8"

FOUNDATION: CRAWLSPACE, UNFINISHED BASEMENT

ORDER ONLINE @ EPLANS.COM

Sullivans Island

A short commute. A lazy holiday. A family gathering place. A rambling porch, gentle breezes, refreshing pink lemonades, and evenings under the stars ... Sullivans Island is the comforting home everyone longs for, especially after having been away too long.

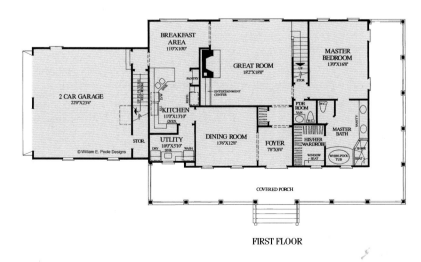

BREAKFAST AREA
11'0"X10'0"

GREAT ROOM
18'2"X18'0"

MASTER BEDROOM
13'0"X16'8"

UP

STOR

2 CAR GARAGE
22'0"X23'4"

PANTRY

ENTERTAINMENT CENTER

REFG

PDR ROOM

VAN

W.C.

KITCHEN
11'0"X13'10"

OVEN

MASTER BATH

VANITY

STOR.

© William E. Poole Designs

UTILITY
10'0"X5'10"

DRY

SINK

WASH

DINING ROOM
13'6"X12'8"

FOYER
7'8"X8'4"

HIS/HER WARDROBE

WINDOW SEAT

WHIRLPOOL TUB

SHWR

SEAT

COVERED PORCH

FIRST FLOOR

Culpeper Cottage

If it's perfect, it can also be simple. And that is exactly what this quaint, shingle-style cottage is. Listening to the excited voices of children as he walks up the path strewn with tricycles, balls, baby dolls, and wagons, it is no wonder that the postman smiles broadly at this charm. The youngsters all rush to him, each eagerly beseeching to be the one to take a letter to mama.

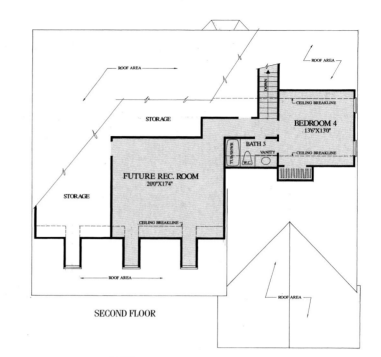

SECOND FLOOR

Second floor labels:
- ROOF AREA
- STORAGE
- BEDROOM 4 13'6"X13'0"
- CEILING BREAKLINE
- BATH 3
- TUB/SHWR
- W.C.
- VANITY
- FUTURE REC. ROOM 20'0"X17'4"
- STORAGE
- CEILING BREAKLINE
- ROOF AREA

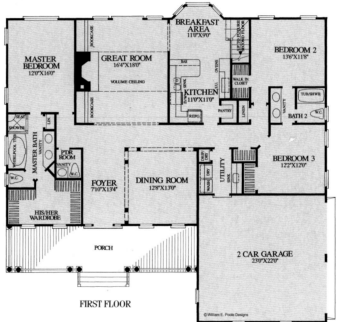

FIRST FLOOR

First floor labels:
- MASTER BEDROOM 12'0"X16'0"
- BOOKCASE
- GREAT ROOM 16'4"X18'0" VOLUME CEILING
- BAR
- BREAKFAST AREA 11'0"X9'0"
- UP TO FUTURE SECOND FLOOR
- BEDROOM 2 13'6"X11'8"
- SINK
- OVEN/S
- WALK IN CLOSET
- SEAT
- SHOWER
- WHIRLPOOL TUB
- MASTER BATH
- VANITY
- LIN.
- KITCHEN 11'0"X11'0"
- D&W/Disp.
- REFG.
- PANTRY
- LINEN
- TUB/SHWR
- BATH 2
- W.C.
- W.C.
- PDR ROOM
- VANITY
- W.C.
- FOYER 7'10"X13'4"
- DINING ROOM 12'8"X13'0"
- WASH
- DRY
- UTILITY
- SINK
- BEDROOM 3 12'2"X12'0"
- HIS/HER WARDROBE
- PORCH
- 2 CAR GARAGE 23'0"X22'0"
- ©William E. Poole Designs, Inc.

© William E. Poole Designs, Inc.

HPK3100015

FIRST FLOOR: 1,981 SQ. FT.
SECOND FLOOR: 291 SQ. FT.
TOTAL: 2,272 SQ. FT.
BONUS SPACE: 412 SQ. FT.
BEDROOMS: 4
BATHROOMS: 3½
WIDTH: 58' - 0"
DEPTH: 53' - 0"
FOUNDATION: Crawlspace

ORDER ONLINE @ EPLANS.COM

HPK3100016

SQUARE FOOTAGE: 1,942
BONUS SPACE: 1,040 SQ. FT.
BEDROOMS: 3
BATHROOMS: 2½
WIDTH: 64' - 10"
DEPTH: 58' - 2"
FOUNDATION: CRAWLSPACE, UNFINISHED BASEMENT

ORDER ONLINE @ EPLANS.COM

Periwinkle

The warmth of home for me and for you is within our hearts 'mid skies of blue. One cannot help but smile when passing by the Periwinkle Cottage. It sparkles. It glows. It is loved for all to see and—means "home" to me.

SECOND FLOOR

FIRST FLOOR

HPK3100017

FIRST FLOOR: 1,554 SQ. FT.

SECOND FLOOR: 755 SQ. FT.

TOTAL: 2,309 SQ. FT.

BONUS SPACE: 869 SQ. FT.

BEDROOMS: 3

BATHROOMS: 2½

WIDTH: 57' - 4"

DEPTH: 39' - 6"

FOUNDATION: Finished Walkout Basement

ORDER ONLINE @ EPLANS.COM

SECOND FLOOR

FIRST FLOOR

Currituck Cottage

He was 10 years old that first summer at the coast. When the tide was low he could walk all the way to the legendary Rock, examining small sea creatures trapped in the tidepools. Other times he ran along the high bluffs or dreamed of pirates and sailing ships. The coastal surroundings of his childhood had a profound effect on his career, and he became one of the greatest artists of our time. Artistic demands have extended his travels, but he has never found a place he'd rather be. Currituck Cottage—a home he's comfortable in.

HELPFUL HINT! Remember: You'll need copies of your plan for your builder, contractors, building department, and you!

Adirondack

The large old Adirondack camps were the inspiration for this exquisite Adirondack cottage. The sensitive use of twig design is delicately detailed in this lovely home. So right in the mountains, so right in the farmlands, so right in any setting where it can blend with the surrounding beauty of nature itself.

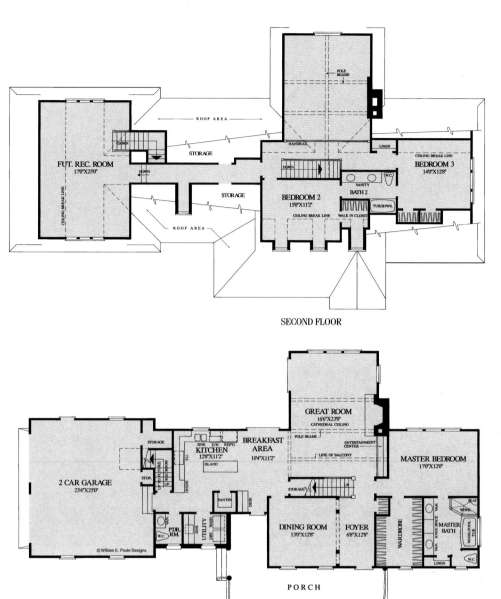

SECOND FLOOR

FUT. REC. ROOM
17'0"X25'0"

STORAGE

ROOF AREA

STORAGE

ROOF AREA

DOWN

DOWN

HANDRAIL

DOWN

LINEN

BEDROOM 3
14'0"X12'8"

CEILING BREAK LINE

VANITY

W.C.

BATH 2

BEDROOM 2
15'0"X11'2"

CEILING BREAK LINE

WALK IN CLOSET

TUB/SHWR.

POLE BEAMS

CEILING BREAK LINE

FIRST FLOOR

2 CAR GARAGE
23'4"X25'0"

STORAGE

STOR.

UP TO FUTURE REC ROOM

UP

SINK D.W. REF'G.

KITCHEN
12'0"X11'2"

ISLAND

OVENS

BREAKFAST AREA
10'4"X11'2"

GREAT ROOM
16'6"X23'0"
CATHEDRAL CEILING

POLE BEAMS

ENTERTAINMENT CENTER

LINE OF BALCONY

MASTER BEDROOM
17'0"X12'0"

PANTRY

DESK

STORAGE

UP

W.C.
P'DR. RM.

SINK
UTILITY
DRY WASH

DINING ROOM
13'0"X12'8"

FOYER
6'8"X12'8"

WARDROBE

VAN. KNEE SPACE VAN.

SEAT

SHWR.

MASTER BATH

WHIRLPOOL TUB

LINEN

W.C.

© William E. Poole Designs

PORCH

HPK3100018

First Floor: 1,712 sq. ft.

Second Floor: 668 sq. ft.

Total: 2,380 sq. ft.

Bonus Space: 573 sq. ft.

Bedrooms: 3

Bathrooms: 2½

Width: 86' - 0"

Depth: 50' - 2"

Foundation: Crawlspace, Unfinished Basement

ORDER ONLINE @ EPLANS.COM

Somerset

As a child she made up stories. Summers were spent gazing at the sky, creating cloud pictures and stories to go with them. The wind presented an ever-changing canvas, transforming the billowing clouds from one image to another. The stories penned in her child-scrawl were packed away, but as a young woman, she never lost her dream of becoming an author. Today, she lingers over a cup of tea in the breakfast room, her mind developing the plot for her latest novel. Dreams do come true in the Somerset—her home.

BRICK PLANTER

DOWN

DECK

W.C.

MASTER
BATH

WHIRLPOOL
TUB

MASTER
BEDROOM
13'0"X17'0"

SHOWER

LINEN

WARDROBE

FOLD
DN.
LB.

UTILITY

STORAGE

DRY WASH SINK

SINK D.W. REF'G.

S.T.L.

ISLAND

SINK

BREAKFAST
AREA
10'10"X14'6"

ENTERTAINMENT
CENTER

FAMILY ROOM
16'8"X19'0"
TRAY CEILING

BEDROOM 2
14'10"X12'0"

KITCHEN
14'0"X14'6"

OVENS

BROOM

PANTRY

DESK

LINENS

WARDROBE

BATH 3

W.C.

TUB/SHWR.

2-CAR GARAGE
23'8"X22'0"

DINING ROOM
12'6"X13'0"

LIVING ROOM
12'0"X16'2"

BEDROOM 3
12'0"X11'8"

BATH 2

W.C.

TUB/SHWR.

FOYER

©William E. Poole Designs

P O R C H

HPK3100019

SQUARE FOOTAGE: 2,394
BEDROOMS: 3
BATHROOMS: 3
WIDTH: 82' - 6"
DEPTH: 52' - 8"
FOUNDATION: CRAWLSPACE

ORDER ONLINE @ EPLANS.COM

HPK3100020

FIRST FLOOR: 1,832 SQ. FT.

SECOND FLOOR: 574 SQ. FT.

TOTAL: 2,406 SQ. FT.

BONUS SPACE: 410 SQ. FT.

BEDROOMS: 4

BATHROOMS: 3

WIDTH: 77' - 10"

DEPTH: 41' - 4"

FOUNDATION: Crawlspace

ORDER ONLINE @ EPLANS.COM

SECOND FLOOR

Santee River House

Whenever will we return with glee, to our beloved home, the Santee? It has been a long trip to the Italian coast, and although the Mediterranean was delightful, dotted with whitewashed villas and the fragrance of decadent seafood dishes, we long for the simple comforts of home. Swinging in the Southern breeze on a wide front porch, the taste of a Low Country boil, and children playing in the lush green grass all conjure up images of home. Oh, how I long for my familiar Southern coast. Italian breezes, carry me home to Santee.

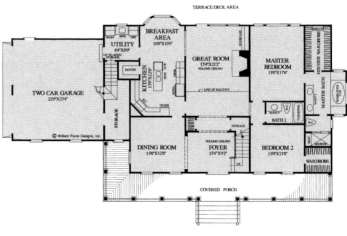

FIRST FLOOR

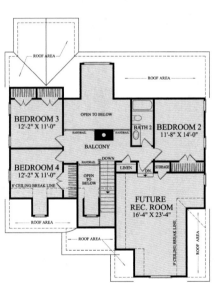

ROOF AREA

ROOF AREA

BEDROOM 3
12'-2" X 11'-0"

OPEN TO BELOW

HANDRAIL   HANDRAIL

BATH 2

BEDROOM 2
11'-8" X 14'-0"

BALCONY

BEDROOM 4
12'-2" X 11'-0"

HANDRAIL

DOWN

LINEN

DN

STORAGE

8' CEILING BREAK LINE

OPEN TO BELOW

FUTURE
REC. ROOM
16'-4" X 23'-4"

ROOF AREA

ROOF AREA

ROOF AREA

9' CEILING BREAK LINE

ROOF AREA

SECOND FLOOR

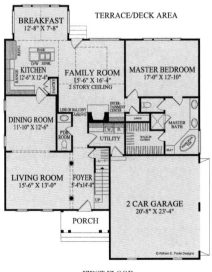

TERRACE/DECK AREA

BREAKFAST
12'-8" X 7'-8"

BAR

D/W SINK

KITCHEN
12'-6" X 12'-4"

RANGE

PANTRY

FAMILY ROOM
15'-6" X 16'-4"
2 STORY CEILING

MASTER BEDROOM
17'-0" X 12'-10"

ENTER-
TAINMENT
CENTER

DINING ROOM
11'-10" X 12'-6"

LINE OF BALCONY
ABOVE

PDR.
ROOM

W. D.

UTILITY

LINEN

WALK-IN
CLOSET

MASTER
BATH

SEAT

LIVING ROOM
15'-6" X 13'-0"

FOYER
5'-4" X 14'-0"

UP

2 CAR GARAGE
20'-8" X 23'-4"

PORCH

© William E. Poole Designs

FIRST FLOOR

Capeville

"One hundred bottles of beer on the wall, 100 bottles of beer" … over and over this rhyme rang out until the sting of salt air overcame our senses. The volume of the verse countdown noticeably diminished when the children saw water beyond the bridge. Simultaneously, all cares of the week before receded as my wife and I settled back for a long weekend of fun and romance at Capeville, our home by the sea.

Blackberry Lane

This "little jewel" of a home emanates a warmth and joy not soon to be forgotten. Cozy, sunlit rooms filled with freshly cut flowers, smiling faces, and the laughter of friends and family abound in the Blackberry Lane. Curved gables, wide trim, stone and shingle siding, and colorful window boxes combined with absolutely perfect proportions truly make this home a neighborhood classic.

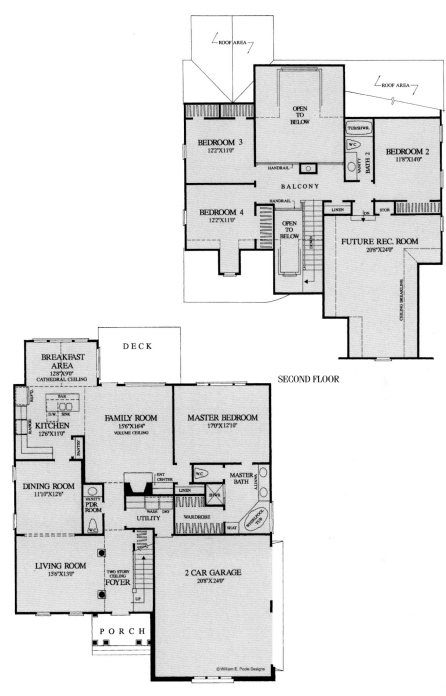

ROOF AREA

ROOF AREA

OPEN TO BELOW

BEDROOM 3
12'2"X11'0"

TUB/SHWR.
W C
VANITY
BATH 2

BEDROOM 2
11'8"X14'0"

HANDRAIL

BALCONY

BEDROOM 4
12'2"X11'0"

HANDRAIL

LINEN
DN.
STOR

OPEN TO BELOW

DOWN

FUTURE REC. ROOM
20'8"X24'0"

CEILING BREAKLINE

SECOND FLOOR

DECK

BREAKFAST AREA
12'8"X9'0"
CATHEDRAL CEILING

BAR
D.W. SINK
REFG.
RANGE

KITCHEN
12'6"X11'0"

PANTRY

FAMILY ROOM
15'6"X16'4"
VOLUME CEILING

MASTER BEDROOM
17'0"X12'10"

W.C.

ENT CENTER

DINING ROOM
11'10"X12'6"

VANITY
P'DR ROOM
W.C.

LINEN

MASTER BATH
VANITY

SHWR

WARDROBE
SEAT
WHIRLPOOL TUB

WASH DRY

UTILITY

LIVING ROOM
15'6"X13'0"

TWO STORY CEILING
FOYER

UP

2 CAR GARAGE
20'8"X24'0"

© William E. Poole Designs

PORCH

FIRST FLOOR

HPK3100022

FIRST FLOOR: 1,627 SQ. FT.

SECOND FLOOR: 783 SQ. FT.

TOTAL: 2,410 SQ. FT.

BONUS SPACE: 418 SQ. FT.

BEDROOMS: 4

BATHROOMS: 2½

WIDTH: 46' - 0"

DEPTH: 58' - 6"

FOUNDATION: CRAWLSPACE

ORDER ONLINE @ EPLANS.COM

Carolina Coastal

Restoration is afoot. Charming cottages being refurbished with loving care abound. However, if the idea of restoration is not your "cup of tea," so to speak, the Carolina Coastal cottage is just for you. Built correctly, it will stand the test of time—just as well as those that came before it. Enjoy!

© William E. Poole Designs, Inc

SECOND FLOOR

FUTURE REC. ROOM
15'0"X22'0"

DOWN

STOR.

ROOF AREA

OPEN TO BELOW

HANDRAIL

BEDROOM 4
12'0"X13'4"

BEDROOM 3
13'0"X14'8"

BALCONY

BATH 3
VANITY

LIN

TUB/SHWR.

DOWN

CEILING BREAK LINE

STOR.

OPEN TO BELOW

STOR.

STOR.

ROOF AREA

FIRST FLOOR

2 CAR GARAGE
22'8"X22'0"

STORAGE

STOR.

UTILITY

DRY. WASH.

PORCH

PANTRY

BREAKFAST AREA
12'0"X11'0"

OPEN TO ABOVE

S.U.

KITCHEN
10'0"X12'0"

DW

SINK

GREAT ROOM
15'4"X21'0"
VAULTED CEILING

OVEN

REFG.

LINE OF BALCONY

MASTER BEDROOM
13'0"X15'8"

HIS/HER WARDROBE

MASTER BATH

WHIRLPOOL TUB

W.C.

VANITY

SHWR.

SEAT

W.C.

DINING ROOM
14'0"X12'8"

STOR.

ARCHED OPENING

FOYER
VAULTED CEILING

UP

LINEN

BATH 2

VANITY

TUB/SHWR.

BEDROOM 2
13'0"X12'8"

© William E. Poole Designs

PORCH

HPK3100023

FIRST FLOOR: 1,776 SQ. FT.

SECOND FLOOR: 643 SQ. FT.

TOTAL: 2,419 SQ. FT.

BONUS SPACE: 367 SQ. FT.

BEDROOMS: 4

BATHROOMS: 3

WIDTH: 61' - 8"

DEPTH: 74' - 4"

FOUNDATION: Crawlspace, Unfinished Basement

ORDER ONLINE @ EPLANS.COM

Hollyhock Cottage

After spending the day in New Bern, North Carolina, touring Tryon Palace and larger homes in the historic district, the most pleasant surprise was waiting just around the corner. We were captivated by the sight of the Holly Hock Cottage. The proportions were perfect, the size adorable, the simplicity engaging, and the gardens ablaze in irregular charm and color. Feasting our eyes on this little cottage at the end of our stay was an unexpected and heartwarming delight.

© William E. Poole Designs, Inc.

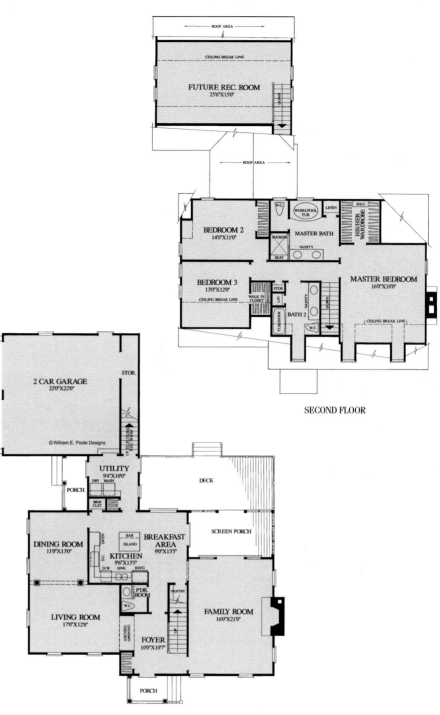

ROOF AREA

CEILING BREAK LINE

FUTURE REC. ROOM
25'6"X15'0"

DOWN

ROOF AREA

W.C.

WHIRLPOOL
TUB

LINEN

SHLV

HIS/HER
WARDROBE

BEDROOM 2
14'0"X11'0"

MASTER BATH

SHOWER

VANITY

SEAT

BEDROOM 3
13'0"X12'0"

STOR

CEILING BREAK LINE

WALK IN
CLOSET

LIN

SHLV

MASTER BEDROOM
16'0"X18'0"

TUB/SHWR

VANITY

BATH 2

DOWN

W.C.

CEILING BREAK LINE

SECOND FLOOR

STOR.

2 CAR GARAGE
22'0"X22'0"

© William E. Poole Designs

UP

REC. ROOM

UTILITY
9'4"X10'0"

DECK

PORCH

DRY

WASH

BRM
CLST

DINING ROOM
11'0"X13'0"

BAR

ISLAND

BREAKFAST
AREA
9'0"X13'5"

SCREEN PORCH

KITCHEN
9'6"X13'5"

D/W

SINK

REFG

PANTRY

LIVING ROOM
17'0"X12'8"

VANITY

P'DR.
ROOM

W.C.

ARCHED
OPENING

FAMILY ROOM
16'0"X21'0"

FOYER
10'0"X10'7"

PORCH

FIRST FLOOR

HPK3100024

FIRST FLOOR: 1,345 SQ. FT.

SECOND FLOOR: 1,088 SQ. FT.

TOTAL: 2,433 SQ. FT.

BONUS SPACE: 410 SQ. FT.

BEDROOMS: 3

BATHROOMS: 2½

WIDTH: 53' - 8"

DEPTH: 67' - 8"

FOUNDATION: CRAWLSPACE, UNFINISHED BASEMENT

ORDER ONLINE @ EPLANS.COM

Edisto River Cottage

What if you could spend summers by the water? Or better yet, live there year-round. The Edisto River Cottage is designed to meet both these needs and meet them well. The front porch lends itself to rocking chairs and storytelling. This is especially enjoyable after playing a game of hide and seek with neighborhood friends and then—best of all—having a sleepover upstairs where whispers and laughter are not easily detected by the grown-ups all tucked safely into their beds below.

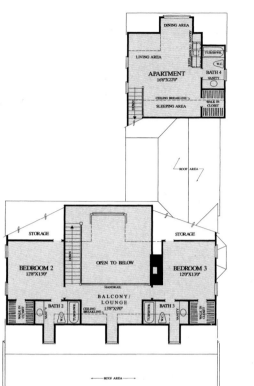

SECOND FLOOR

FIRST FLOOR

Camden

The Camden is the home that everyone wants to possess—the one in the neighborhood that never needs to be advertised for sale. Why? Because all of your friends have said, "John, if you even think about selling your home, please call me first." And of course, you do. The Camden welcomes each new family to its hearth with the warmth and glow of home—that special place where the heart is.

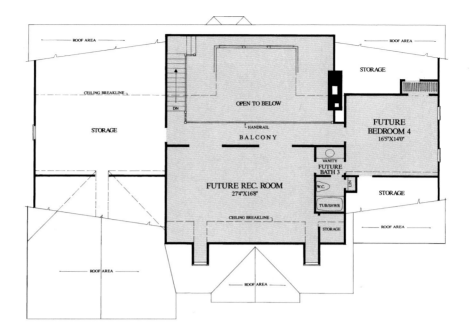

ROOF AREA — ROOF AREA

STORAGE

CEILING BREAKLINE

OPEN TO BELOW

STORAGE

FUTURE
BEDROOM 4
16'5"X14'0"

DN

HANDRAIL

BALCONY

VANITY

FUTURE
BATH 3

STORAGE

FUTURE REC. ROOM
27'4"X16'8"

W.C

LIN

TUB/SHWR

STORAGE

CEILING BREAKLINE

ROOF AREA

ROOF AREA

ROOF AREA

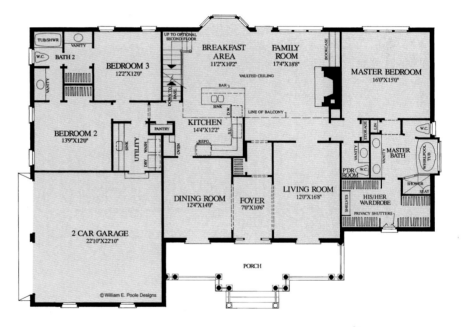

TUB/SHWR

VANITY

W.C

BATH 2

VANITY

BEDROOM 3
12'2"X12'0"

UP TO OPTIONAL
SECOND FLOOR

DOWN TO
BASE

BREAKFAST
AREA
11'2"X10'2"

FAMILY
ROOM
17'4"X18'8"

BOOKCASE

MASTER BEDROOM
16'0"X15'0"

VAULTED CEILING

BAR

SINK

BEDROOM 2
13'9"X12'0"

PANTRY

KITCHEN
14'4"X12'2"

D.W

LINE OF BALCONY

SINK

UTILITY

DRY WASH

OVEN

REFG.

STORAGE

LIN

W.C

VANITY

MASTER
BATH

WHIRLPOOL TUB

2 CAR GARAGE
22'10"X22'10"

DINING ROOM
12'4"X14'0"

FOYER
7'0"X10'6"

LIVING ROOM
12'0"X16'8"

P'DR
ROOM

W.C

VANITY

SHELVES

HIS/HER
WARDROBE

SHOWER

SEAT

PRIVACY SHUTTERS

© William E. Poole Designs

PORCH

HPK3100026

SQUARE FOOTAGE: 2,441

BONUS SPACE: 606 SQ. FT.

BEDROOMS: 3

BATHROOMS: 2½

WIDTH: 74' - 0"

DEPTH: 51' - 0"

FOUNDATION: CRAWLSPACE, UNFINISHED BASEMENT

ORDER ONLINE @ EPLANS.COM

Gulf Coast Cottage

Breathtaking sunsets. Sultry summer nights. The glow of the moon and starry, starry skies—romance. Fireflies glowing in the dark, children playing in the park, the warmth of a hand holding mine, the tenderness of a first kiss— all the joys of a lifetime remembered from the porch of the Gulf Coast Cottage.

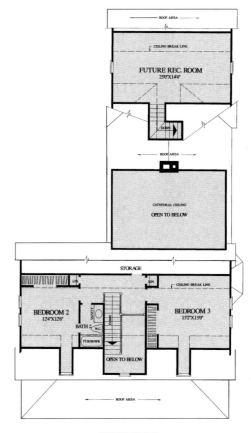

SECOND FLOOR

Future Rec. Room 25'0"X14'4"

Bedroom 2 12'4"X12'6"

Bedroom 3 15'2"X15'0"

2 CAR GARAGE 25'0"X22'0"

©William E. Poole Designs

UTILITY 12'8"X7'4"

Great Room 24'0"X18'4"

Master Bedroom 17'8"X14'4"

Breakfast Area 9'6"X13'0"

Kitchen 10'2"X13'0"

Master Bath

Foyer 8'8"X12'0"

Dining Room 16'4"X12'0"

Covered Porch

FIRST FLOOR

HPK3100027

First Floor: 1,819 sq. ft.

Second Floor: 638 sq. ft.

Total: 2,457 sq. ft.

Bonus Space: 385 sq. ft.

Bedrooms: 3

Bathrooms: 2½

Width: 47' - 4"

Depth: 82' - 8"

Foundation: Crawlspace, Unfinished Basement

ORDER ONLINE @ EPLANS.COM

HPK3100028

First Floor: 1,365 SQ. FT.

Second Floor: 1,120 SQ. FT.

Total: 2,485 SQ. FT.

Bonus Space: 506 SQ. FT.

Bedrooms: 3

Bathrooms: 2½

Width: 49' - 8"

Depth: 64' - 0"

Foundation: Crawlspace, Unfinished Basement

ORDER ONLINE @ EPLANS.COM

Colonial Cottage

An American tradition—that is what our Colonial Cottage is. No two are ever exactly alike, yet a similarity of classical details exists that strongly ties these cottages together. Try one on for size—reveal the inner you. You'll be glad you did.

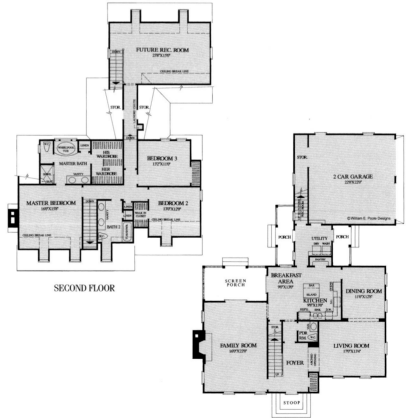

SECOND FLOOR

FIRST FLOOR

©1993 William E Poole Designs, Inc.

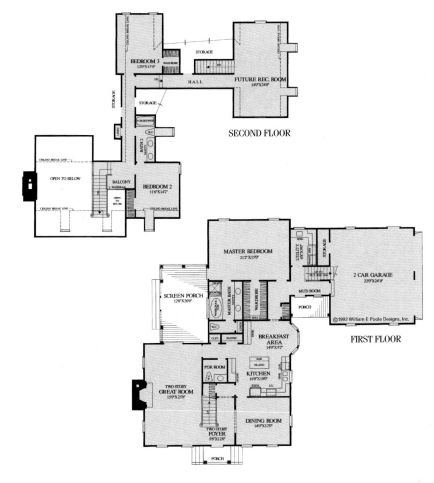

SECOND FLOOR

FIRST FLOOR

©1993 William E Poole Designs, Inc.

HPK3100029

FIRST FLOOR: 1,884 SQ. FT.

SECOND FLOOR: 661 SQ. FT.

TOTAL: 2,545 SQ. FT.

BONUS SPACE: 489 SQ. FT.

BEDROOMS: 3

BATHROOMS: 2½

WIDTH: 71' - 4"

DEPTH: 62' - 2"

FOUNDATION: Crawlspace

ORDER ONLINE @ EPLANS.COM

Williamsburg Cottage

Visiting Williamsburg is not something to do just once, but many times. As we left the King's Arms Tavern one Halloween evening, we saw children "trick or treating" along Duke of Gloucester Street. The only illumination was from candlelit pumpkins placed at every gateway. The perfect balance of the homes (with no two alike): the simple straightforward approach to architecture: the welcoming and humanizing feeling that pervades, along with a sense of time and place—all bespeak the warmth of home

HPK3100030

FIRST FLOOR: 1,883 SQ. FT.

SECOND FLOOR: 803 SQ. FT.

TOTAL: 2,686 SQ. FT.

BONUS SPACE: 489 SQ. FT.

BEDROOMS: 3

BATHROOMS: 3½

WIDTH: 63' - 0"

DEPTH: 81' - 10"

FOUNDATION: Crawlspace

ORDER ONLINE @ EPLANS.COM

Battery Creek Cottage

Where creeks converge and marsh grasses sway in gentle breezes, the Battery Creek Cottage is a classical low-country home. Steep rooflines, high ceilings, front and back porches, plus long and low windows are typical details of these charming planter's cottages. Spanish moss, alligators, and horseflies go with the local scenery, too. However, this pleasant and cozy home illustrates a way of life that crosses regional boundaries and looks great anywhere. We just can't export the 'gators.

FIRST FLOOR

SECOND FLOOR

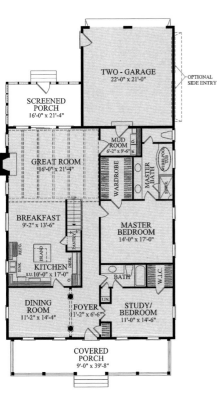

FIRST FLOOR

SCREENED PORCH
16'-0" x 21'-4"

TWO - GARAGE
22'-0" x 21'-0"

OPTIONAL SIDE ENTRY

GREAT ROOM
16'-0" x 21'-4"

MUD ROOM
6'-2" x 9'-6"

WARDROBE

MASTER BATH

BREAKFAST
9'-2" x 13'-6"

MASTER BEDROOM
14'-0" x 17'-0"

KITCHEN
s.u. 10'-0" x 17'-0"

ISLAND

PANTRY

DESK

REFG.

SINK

W.I.C.

BATH

DINING ROOM
11'-2" x 14'-4"

FOYER
11'-2" x 6'-6"

STUDY/ BEDROOM
11'-0" x 14'-6"

LIN.

COVERED PORCH
9'-0" x 39'-8"

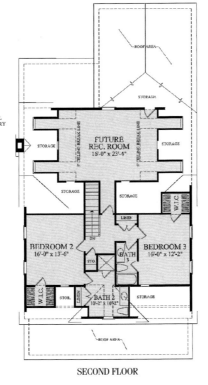

SECOND FLOOR

ROOF AREA

STORAGE

FUTURE REC. ROOM
15'-0" x 23'-4"

STORAGE

STORAGE

STORAGE

STORAGE

STORAGE

W.I.C.

BEDROOM 2
16'-0" x 13'-6"

DN

LINEN

BATH 3

BEDROOM 3
16'-0" x 12'-2"

STO.

W.I.C.

STOR.

LINEN

BATH 2
10'-2" x 10'-2"

STORAGE

ROOF AREA

HPK3100031

FIRST FLOOR: 1,904 SQ. FT.

SECOND FLOOR: 819 SQ. FT.

TOTAL: 2,723 SQ. FT.

BEDROOMS: 4

BATHROOMS: 4

WIDTH: 39' - 8"

DEPTH: 78' - 8"

FOUNDATION: CRAWLSPACE

ORDER ONLINE @ EPLANS.COM

The Sweetbriar

The Sweetbriar is an adorable cottage that literally beckons one to come up, sit in the swing, and swap tales of adventures had and dreams of those yet to come. It reminds us of our Great Aunt's home and touches our hearts in such a way that we want to make it our very own. A place to remember the old and create the new—memories to last a lifetime or two.

Classic Hometown Designs

BELOW: A classic look for any location: twin dormers atop a full-width, covered front porch. RIGHT: A clerestory window lights the family room from above. Built-ins beside the central fireplace provide extra storage and display space.

Bayou Cottage
Recall a favorite childhood home with one of these timeless, neighborhood-friendly designs

Down in Louisiana, the home style has a high foundation, sweeping roof, covered porch, and French-inspired details; in Massachusetts, the Cape Cod has a steeply-pitched side-gable, dormers, and a central fireplace. Each is unique in its origins, but both evoke a feeling of community and days gone by. This neighborhood home may be typical along the Gulf Coast, but it can also rest on the streets of Florida, on the coasts of the Carolinas, or among the pine trees of New England. The plans in "Classic Hometown Designs" are universally appealing and can be at home in any neighborhood—such as yours.

This home uses a Cajun influence to suit its Louisiana surroundings. The floor plan is designed to make the most of summer breezes and crosswinds, when the climate is at its most humid. A wide front porch welcomes evenings spent enjoying cooler air. Two front dormers increase square footage of the second floor and decorate the hipped roofline.

Down in Louisiana, where the jambalaya, catfish stew, and spicy Cajun food are so delightfully savored, the homes are equally unique and enjoyable.

Classic Hometown Designs

Sunlight streams through a window in the
master bedroom, keeping the room well-lit;
warm draperies and a thoughtful layout keep
the room cozy and secluded.

A front-facing dining room accommodates
guests on special occasions. Hardwood
floors and colorful window treatments
make the room formal yet friendly.

Enter the foyer, with a staircase flanked by the living and dining rooms that leads up to three bedrooms, two baths, and a bonus future rec room. Straight ahead, a family room features a fireplace, with built-ins on either side, and a brilliant clerestory window. The kitchen is light and airy with a naturally lit breakfast nook. The first-floor master bedroom also has a wide window, but an accommodating master bath with double vanity, tub, shower, and compartmented toilet ensure privacy. The L-shaped walk-in closet has room for his clothes, her clothes, and then some.

Formal and informal spaces in these neighborhood favorites make sure the needs of every occasion are met, while dormers and porches recall the timeless homes of youth. Browse through this section to find your own Classic Hometown Design. ∎

Serve casual meals easily with an open, island kitchen adjacent to the breakfast area.

HPK3100032

FIRST FLOOR: 2,142 SQ. FT.
SECOND FLOOR: 960 SQ. FT.
TOTAL: 3,102 SQ. FT.
BONUS SPACE: 327 SQ. FT.
BEDROOMS: 4
BATHROOMS: 3½
WIDTH: 75' - 8"
DEPTH: 53' - 0"
FOUNDATION: Crawlspace

ORDER ONLINE @ EPLANS.COM

FIRST FLOOR

SECOND FLOOR

HPK3100033

First Floor: 2,000 sq. ft.

Second Floor: 1,062 sq. ft.

Total: 3,062 sq. ft.

Bonus Space: 529 sq. ft.

Bedrooms: 4

Bathrooms: 3½

Width: 79' - 10"

Depth: 52' - 4"

Foundation: Crawlspace

ORDER ONLINE @ EPLANS.COM

SECOND FLOOR

FIRST FLOOR

The Berry Hill

In many areas of the Lower South during the early 19th century, French and Spanish influences blended to form a unique house type. The Berry Hill, a typical Mississippi River Delta planters cottage, is a beautiful interpretation of those historic dwellings. Rather than basing this plan on one historic residence, William Poole designed the house to be composite of vernacular architectural elements found along the rivers and bayous of the Lower South. A slightly raised foundation helps keep this climate-conscious house cool and dry. A simple balustrade spans the front of the house, and sic Doric columns support the deep, overhanging porch. Sidelights and an elliptical transom dress the front door. Tall breeze-catching windows on the lower level combine with round-top windows in the dormers to further enhance the regional look.

HELPFUL HINT! Our custom modification service can add a walk-out basement to any plan—great for hillside lots!

Back Bay Cottage

Near Edisto Island, South Carolina, small backwater communities filled with low-country cottages are dotted here, there, and everywhere. Some have manicured lawns. Some have finely raked patterns in the bare, sandy soil. Some are freshly painted. Some are so weathered that they appear never to have known the art of cosmetic covering. However, all are abundantly filled with the colors and fragrances of beautiful flowers. There is no doubt that these homes are old with many a story to tell, and they are clearly so well loved and cared for (whatever the circumstances of their owners) that although these cottages bespeak country, it is with quiet and genteel sophistication.

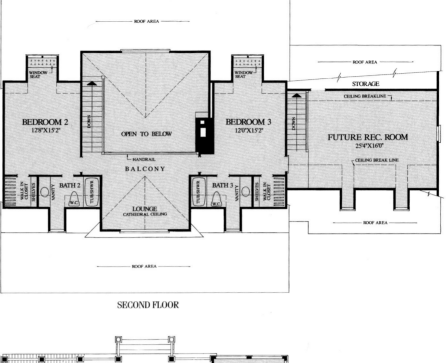

SECOND FLOOR

Second floor labels:
- WINDOW SEAT
- BEDROOM 2 12'8"X15'2"
- OPEN TO BELOW
- DOWN
- HANDRAIL
- BALCONY
- WALK IN CLOSET
- SHELVES
- VANITY
- BATH 2
- TUB/SHWR
- W.C.
- LOUNGE CATHEDRAL CEILING
- ROOF AREA
- WINDOW SEAT
- BEDROOM 3 12'0"X15'2"
- TUB/SHWR
- BATH 3
- W.C.
- VANITY
- SHELVES
- WALK IN CLOSET
- ROOF AREA
- STORAGE
- CEILING BREAKLINE
- FUTURE REC. ROOM 25'4"X16'0"
- CEILING BREAK LINE
- DOWN
- ROOF AREA

FIRST FLOOR

First floor labels:
- PORCH
- BREAKFAST AREA 12'0"X12'0"
- UTILITY
- DRY WASH
- DRIP/DRY
- STORAGE
- MASTER BEDROOM 12'8"X18'0"
- UP
- WALK IN CLOSET
- GREAT ROOM CATHEDRAL CEILING 18'4"X23'8"
- ENTERTAINMENT CENTER
- BAR
- D/W
- KITCHEN 12'0"X13'2"
- REFG
- PANTRY
- OVEN
- S.I.
- UP TO FUTURE REC. ROOM
- 2 CAR GARAGE 25'4"X22'0"
- WARDROBE
- MASTER BATH
- VANITY
- LINE OF BALCONY
- LINEN
- SEAT
- SHOWER
- WHIRLPOOL TUB
- PRIVACY SHUTTERS
- SHELVES
- ARCHED OPENING
- FOYER 8'2"X5'0"
- SHELVES
- VANITY
- W.C.
- P'DR ROOM
- DINING ROOM 14'4"X12'6"
- WORKBENCH
- © William E. Poole Designs
- PORCH

The Beaufort II

In North Carolina, there is a little seafaring town filled with the charm and antiquity of the 18th Century. One of the old homes of West Indies influence, The Beaufort II has been lovingly restored by a noted writer of fiction. Considered by some to be a mystery himself, he wanders about at night in the mists and delights in the eerie noises of ships echoing throughout the harbor. From these solitary musings comes the stuff that books are made of. We are left to wonder, what next...

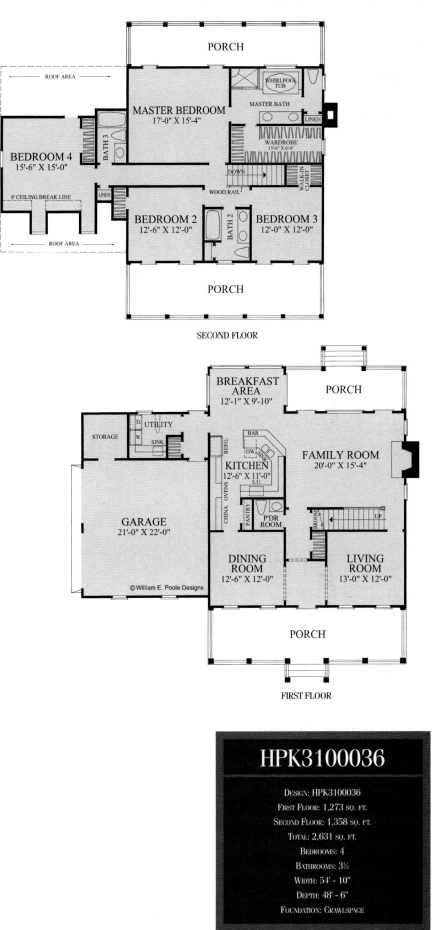

SECOND FLOOR

PORCH

ROOF AREA

MASTER BEDROOM
17'-0" X 15'-4"

MASTER BATH

WHIRLPOOL TUB

LINEN

WARDROBE
15'-6" X 6'-0"

BATH 3

BEDROOM 4
15'-6" X 15'-0"

DOWN

WALK-IN CLOSET

8' CEILING BREAK LINE

LINEN

WOOD RAIL

ROOF AREA

BEDROOM 2
12'-6" X 12'-0"

BATH 2

BEDROOM 3
12'-0" X 12'-0"

PORCH

FIRST FLOOR

BREAKFAST AREA
12'-1" X 9'-10"

PORCH

STORAGE

UTILITY

D.
W.

SINK

BAR

REFG.

DW
SINK

FAMILY ROOM
20'-0" X 15'-4"

KITCHEN
12'-6" X 11'-0"

S.U.

GARAGE
21'-0" X 22'-0"

CHINA

OVENS

PANTRY

P'DR ROOM

BROOM

UP

©William E. Poole Designs

DINING ROOM
12'-6" X 12'-0"

LIVING ROOM
13'-0" X 12'-0"

PORCH

HPK3100036

DESIGN: HPK3100036

FIRST FLOOR: 1,273 SQ. FT.

SECOND FLOOR: 1,358 SQ. FT.

TOTAL: 2,631 SQ. FT.

BEDROOMS: 4

BATHROOMS: 3½

WIDTH: 54' - 10"

DEPTH: 48' - 6"

FOUNDATION: CRAWLSPACE

ORDER ONLINE @ EPLANS.COM

© William E. Poole Designs, Inc.

HPK3100035

First Floor: 1,291 sq. ft.
Second Floor: 1,087 sq. ft.
Total: 2,378 sq. ft.
Bonus Space: 366 sq. ft.
Bedrooms: 3
Bathrooms: 2½
Width: 65' - 4"
Depth: 40' - 0"
Foundation: Crawlspace

ORDER ONLINE @ EPLANS.COM

Texarkana

No gimmicks, just the real thing—Texarkana is a farmhouse of such handsome proportions that once you see it for the first time, you know for certain that it is meant to be your home. Simple, solid, and secure in its place in the scheme of things, the Texarkana is a favorite place for neighbors to gather in the early evening hours for a friendly game of baseball and hopefully, a special treat of homemade ice cream.

SECOND FLOOR

FIRST FLOOR

© William E. Poole Designs, Inc.

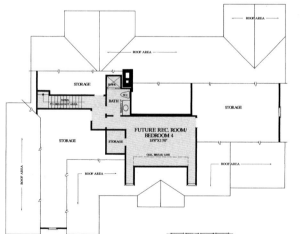

© William E. Poole Designs

HPK3100037

SQUARE FOOTAGE: 2,639

BONUS SPACE: 396 SQ. FT.

BEDROOMS: 3

BATHROOMS: 2½

WIDTH: 73' - 8"

DEPTH: 58' - 6"

FOUNDATION: CRAWLSPACE

ORDER ONLINE @ EPLANS.COM

Albany

Quite often on the way home from school my first stop would be at the doughnut shop. While savoring the delicious hot treat, I would saunter along tree-lined streets, admiring the detailed intricacies of each individual home I passed. One classic (yet warm and inviting) home had special appeal to me then and now. I call it the Albany—a homeplace from my memory for you.

© William E. Poole Designs, Inc.

Lafayette

Let me tell you a little known but very true story. When our soldiers were overseas during World War I, they fell in love with the inviting, aged, and patinaed old homes of France—homes that gave them feelings of warmth in their otherwise desolate days. Upon returning home after the war, they decided to build romantic cottages such as Lafayette for themselves; thus, introducing to our shores the symmetry, quaintness, and detail of classical French architecture. And as all classics do, these homes remain and gracefully endure the test of time.

STORAGE   STORAGE

2 CAR GARAGE
22'0"X22'0"

© William E. Poole Designs

UTILITY
13'0"X8'0"

PDR. ROOM

BREAKFAST
AREA
13'0"X10'0"

KITCHEN
13'0"X12'0"

DINING ROOM
13'0"X15'0"

FAMILY ROOM
21'9"X16'0"
WOOD BEAMS

LIVING ROOM
14'0"X16'0"

FOYER
7'9"X16'0"

BEDROOM 2
14'0"X12'6"

MASTER BEDROOM
15'9"X18'0"

WHIRLPOOL TUB

MASTER BATH
VANITY

BEDROOM 3
13'0"X12'6"

BATH 2

STOOP

ROOF AREA

BEDROOM 5
11'6"X12'2"

FUTURE REC. ROOM
22'8"X19'6"

STOR.   HANDRAIL   STOR.

CLOSET

BEDROOM 4
15'0"X12'2"

BATH 3

ROOF AREA

SECOND FLOOR

ROOF AREA

LINEN

BEDROOM 4
12'0"X12'0"

BATH 3

W.C.

VANITY

TUB/SHWR

OPEN TO BELOW

CEILING BREAK LINE

SITTING AREA
13'0"X10'6"

DOWN

HANDRAIL

LINEN

WALK IN CLOSET

TUB/WB

BEDROOM 3
11'8"X12'0"

W.C.

BEDROOM 2
12'8"X10'0"

BATH 2

VANITY

CEILING BREAK LINE

ROOF AREA

UP

STOR.

COVERED PORCH

ROOF AREA

FUTURE REC ROOM
14'8"X29'0"

CEILING BREAK LINE

FIRST FLOOR

MASTER BEDROOM
16'4"X14'4"

HERS/HER WARDROBE

OPEN TO ABOVE
VAULTED CEILING
FAMILY ROOM
17'8"X14'4"

OPEN TO ABOVE
VAULTED CEILING
BREAKFAST AREA
12'8"X10'8"

MASTER BATH

SEAT
SHOWER

W.C.

VANITY

PDR ROOM

FOLD DN. IR.

WASH

DRY

BAR

KITCHEN
12'8"X11'8"

D.W.

PANTRY

REF/FRZ.

STORAGE

FOYER
4'8"X15'8"

LIVING ROOM
13'0"X15'8"

DINING ROOM
12'8"X11'4"

LINEN

UTILITY
9'6"X10'4"

STORAGE

2 CAR GARAGE
22'8"X22'0"

COVERED PORCH

© William E. Poole Designs

HPK3100039

First Floor: 1,809 sq. ft.
Second Floor: 944 sq. ft.
Total: 2,753 sq. ft.
Bonus Space: 440 sq. ft.
Bedrooms: 4
Bathrooms: 3½
Width: 54' - 4"
Depth: 59' - 0"
Foundation: Crawlspace, Unfinished Basement

ORDER ONLINE @ EPLANS.COM

Cape May

What a charming town. All along the streets sit cottages of exquisite detail—which one shall it be? Which one will shelter us in storms and hold us tenderly throughout our summer days? The Cape May, of course. None other could match its warmth, its intricate design, and its romantic charm.

Carmel Cottage

The winding streets, the quaint little shops, the pounding surf, the trees as far as one can see—the setting for Carmel Cottage. Warm, weathered, and welcoming, this home endures the test of time and embraces all who pause to admire.

STORAGE

ROOF AREA

ROOF AREA

BEDROOM 2
14'0"X15'0"

OPEN TO BELOW

CEILING BREAK LINE

BEDROOM 4
12'0"X10'0"

BATH 2
TUB/SHWR
VANITY
W.C.

HANDRAIL

BALCONY

TUB/SHWR
W.C.

BATH 3
VANITY

STORAGE
LINEN
LIN

FUTURE REC. ROOM
21'8"X23'0"

OPEN TO BELOW

DOWN

BEDROOM 3
13'2"X12'8"

CEILING BREAK LINE

CEILING BREAK LINE

ROOF AREA

SECOND FLOOR

Miles Mceon

BREAKFAST AREA
11'4"X8'8"

ENTERTAINMENT
CENTER

OPEN TO ABOVE

PANTRY

BAR
SINK   D.W.

MASTER BEDROOM
17'0"X13'0"

VAULTED CEILING
FAMILY ROOM
17'8"X18'0"

ISLAND

KITCHEN
12'4"X17'4"

RANGE   OVENS

REFG.

SHOWER

MASTER
BATH

VANITY

LINEN

STOR.

DINING ROOM
12'0"X12'8"

WOOD TRELLIS

WHIRLPOOL
TUB

HIS/HER
WARDROBE

WASH   DRY

UTILITY
7'6"X8'0"

VANITY
PDR
ROOM
W.C.

DINING TERRACE

W.C.

LIN

VAULTED
CEILING
FOYER
9'4"X14'8"

LIVING ROOM
15'4"X13'8"

STUCCO WALL

2 CAR GARAGE
21'8"X23'0"

UP

PORCH

FIRST FLOOR

© William E. Poole Designs

STORAGE

HPK3100040

FIRST FLOOR: 1,805 SQ. FT.

SECOND FLOOR: 952 SQ. FT.

TOTAL: 2,757 SQ. FT.

BONUS SPACE: 475 SQ. FT.

BEDROOMS: 4

BATHROOMS: 3½

WIDTH: 48' - 10"

DEPTH: 64' - 10"

FOUNDATION: CRAWLSPACE, UNFINISHED BASEMENT

HPK3100041

SQUARE FOOTAGE: 2,777

BONUS SPACE: 424 SQ. FT.

BEDROOMS: 3

BATHROOMS: 2½

WIDTH: 75' - 6"

DEPTH: 60' - 2"

FOUNDATION: CRAWLSPACE, UNFINISHED BASEMENT

Bowling Green

Can you not just see it—sloping green lawns all the way to the river, sprawling wildflower gardens, rose trellises, and white fences galore. Bowling Green, a place to nestle into, a place called home. Children running, playing, calling cheerfully to all who will listen; grown-ups strolling about visiting with one another until, at last, the newlyweds appear for all to toast with good wishes and loving entreaties for their frequent returns to Bowling Green.

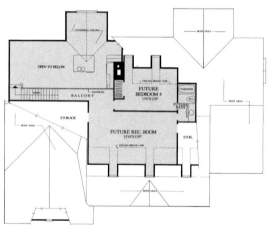

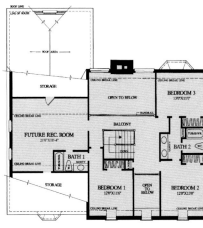

SECOND FLOOR

HPK3100042

First Floor: 1,816 sq. ft.
Second Floor: 968 sq. ft.
Total: 2,784 sq. ft.
Bedrooms: 4
Bathrooms: 3½
Width: 54' - 6"
Depth: 52' - 5"
Foundation: Crawlspace

ORDER ONLINE @ EPLANS.COM

The Leesburg

"The Colonel is home, the Colonel is home," the neighborhood children all shouted as the shining black limousine pulled up to the Leesburg. This was always an exciting time because he told them stories about where he had been and who he had seen in far away places. He also always bought them presents and, while they devoured cookies and milk, kept them entranced with his stories for hours. One could not tell whether his home-comings were enjoyed more by him or the children, for he was as delighted with their attention as they were with his.

FIRST FLOOR

Helpful Hint! All plans in this magazine were drawn by designers working under strict industry standards.

HPK3100043

First Floor: 1,816 sq. ft.

Second Floor: 968 sq. ft.

Total: 2,784 sq. ft.

Bonus Space: 402 sq. ft.

Bedrooms: 4

Bathrooms: 3½

Width: 54' - 6"

Depth: 52' - 8"

Foundation: Crawlspace

ORDER ONLINE @ EPLANS.COM

Arlington

Picnics. Parades. Fireworks. Flags. Fourth of July celebrations. Nowhere are patriotic commemorations more evident than in the areas surrounding our nation's capital. The patina of old brick, the diversity of classical design, and the lushness of mature plantings provide the serenity requisite to these older homes that whisper a fond farewell in the morning and a warm welcome every evening—as the family gathers at home in the Arlington once again.

SECOND FLOOR

FIRST FLOOR

© William E. Poole Designs, Inc.

HPK3100054

SQUARE FOOTAGE: 3,049
BONUS SPACE: 868 SQ. FT.
BEDROOMS: 3
BATHROOMS: 2½
WIDTH: 72' - 6"
DEPTH: 78' - 10"
FOUNDATION: Crawlspace, Unfinished Basement

ORDER ONLINE @ EPLANS.COM

Les Serein

With hair flying and cheeks rosy, the lady of Les Serein pedaled her bicycle through the winding streets of town. Along her travels, greetings were exchanged with passing neighbors as they made their way—as they did every morning— to and from the bakery. In some places, some things never change—nor should they.

Salisbury

In a perfect little Southern town, Aunt Bea of "Mayberry" fame decided to spend the remainder of her life. After living in the imagery of sleepy Southern perfection, she wanted the real thing. This picturesque rendition of our Salisbury is, of course, a perfect fit. We all hope she found exactly what she was looking for.

© William E. Poole Designs, Inc.

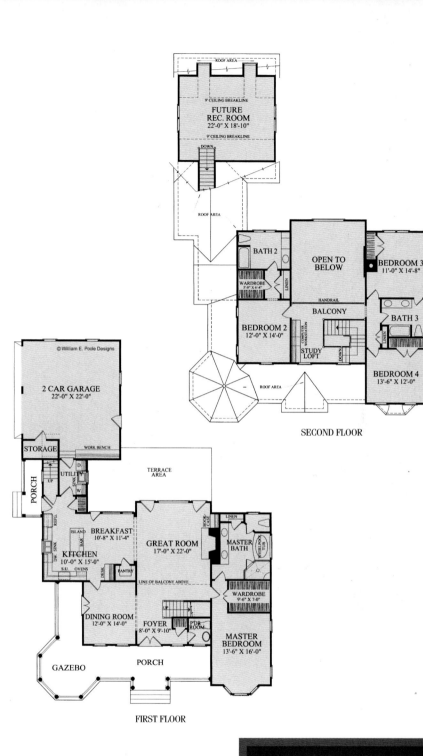

ROOF AREA

9' CEILING BREAKLINE

**FUTURE
REC. ROOM**
22'-0" X 18'-10"

9' CEILING BREAKLINE

DOWN

ROOF AREA

BATH 2

**OPEN TO
BELOW**

BEDROOM 3
11'-0" X 14'-8"

WARDROBE
5'-8" X 6'-4"

LINEN

HANDRAIL

BALCONY

BEDROOM 2
12'-0" X 14'-0"

COMPUTER WORKSTATION

BATH 3

STUDY
LOFT

DOWN

LINEN

ROOF AREA

BEDROOM 4
13'-6" X 12'-0"

SECOND FLOOR

© William E. Poole Designs

2 CAR GARAGE
22'-0" X 22'-0"

STORAGE

WORK BENCH

TERRACE
AREA

PORCH

UP

D.

UTILITY

SINK

W.

BOOKCASE

LINEN

REFR.

ISLAND

BASE

BREAKFAST
10'-8" X 11'-4"

GREAT ROOM
17'-0" X 22'-0"

**MASTER
BATH**

WHIRLPOOL TUB

DW. SINK

KITCHEN
10'-0" X 15'-0"

DESK

PANTRY

S.U.

OVENS

LINE OF BALCONY ABOVE

WARDROBE
9'-6" X 7'-0"

DINING ROOM
12'-0" X 14'-0"

UP

FOYER
8'-0" X 9'-10"

P'DR
ROOM

**MASTER
BEDROOM**
13'-6" X 16'-0"

GAZEBO

PORCH

FIRST FLOOR

GregHavens

HPK3100045

FIRST FLOOR: 1,734 SQ. FT.

SECOND FLOOR: 1,091 SQ. FT.

TOTAL: 2,825 SQ. FT.

BONUS SPACE: 488 SQ. FT.

BEDROOMS: 4

BATHROOMS: 3½

WIDTH: 57' - 6"

DEPTH: 80' - 11"

FOUNDATION: CRAWLSPACE, UNFINISHED BASEMENT

ORDER ONLINE @ EPLANS.COM

HPK3100046

FIRST FLOOR: 1,921 SQ. FT.

SECOND FLOOR: 921 SQ. FT.

TOTAL: 2,842 SQ. FT.

BONUS SPACE: 454 SQ. FT.

BEDROOMS: 4

BATHROOMS: 3½

WIDTH: 62' - 2"

DEPTH: 71' - 0"

FOUNDATION: CRAWLSPACE, UNFINISHED BASEMENT

ORDER ONLINE @ EPLANS.COM

Fieldstone Farm

Oh, I was so humiliated. At the age of seven, with my own pony at Fieldstone Farm, I was certain I could ride the bucking donkey at the fair. Eluding my father's grasp, I slipped quickly toward the clown, who led me around the ring. The donkey bucked not once, yet the "little lady" was offered the five dollar prize. My feelings were hurt. My pride was destroyed. My only recourse was to decline the five dollar bill and return determinedly to my seat.

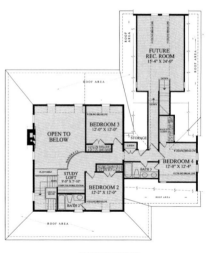

SECOND FLOOR

FIRST FLOOR

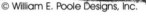

HELPFUL HINT! A predrawn house plan is $8,000–$20,000 cheaper than a typical architect's custom design.

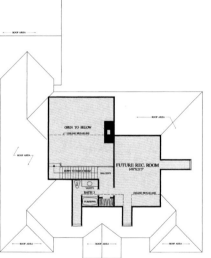

© William E. Poole Designs, Inc.

HPK3100047

SQUARE FOOTAGE: 2,869
BEDROOMS: 3
BATHROOMS: 3½
WIDTH: 68' - 6"
DEPTH: 79' - 8"
FOUNDATION: Crawlspace

ORDER ONLINE @ EPLANS.COM

Vicksburg

Remember when the whole family would go to spend Sunday with relatives? Remember how you held your breath as you approached your destination—how every flower, every blade of grass, every cloud in the sky seemed so right. The Vicksburg is of the architectural style found in old urban neighborhoods throughout the country. This design resists the stereotype. It is perfectly balanced with an open, flowing one-level floor plan for today's lifestyle (bonus space above) with no sacrifice of classical architecture.

Homestead

Rounding a curve near the Blue Ridge Parkway—there, straight ahead, nestled between adjacent ridges lies the Homestead. With a sudden catch in the throat, one is immediately immersed in images of the generations who have lived, loved, and toiled there. Lullabies, folk tales, and the clear lilt of a fiddle in the crisp evening air invade one's senses in a rush of nostalgic reverie. Imagine the stories that could be told!

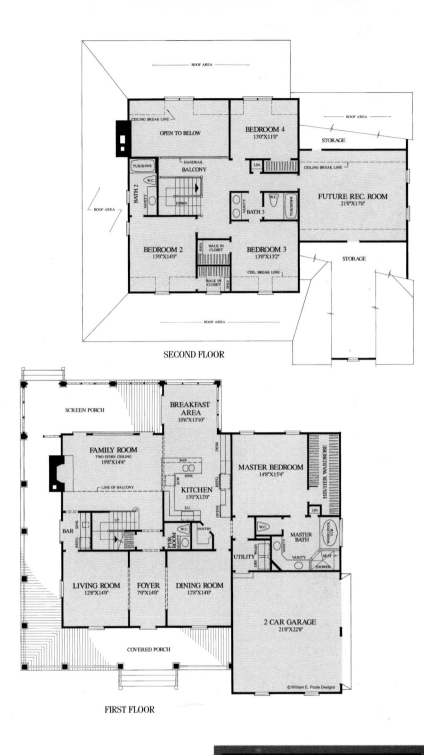

SECOND FLOOR

FIRST FLOOR

© William E. Poole Designs

HPK3100048

FIRST FLOOR: 1,913 SQ. FT.

SECOND FLOOR: 997 SQ. FT.

TOTAL: 2,910 SQ. FT.

BONUS SPACE: 377 SQ. FT.

BEDROOMS: 4

BATHROOMS: 3½

WIDTH: 63' - 0"

DEPTH: 59' - 4"

FOUNDATION: CRAWLSPACE, UNFINISHED BASEMENT

ORDER ONLINE @ EPLANS.COM

Virginia Farmhouse

It has been said that there is a reason for all things and that for all things there is a season. The original farmhouses were of local materials and well-balanced. The porches provided shade and shelter, the dormers provided light in the upper half-story, and the season for this Virginia Farmhouse is—forever.

© William E. Poole Designs, Inc.

SECOND FLOOR

FIRST FLOOR

HPK3100050

FIRST FLOOR: 2,014 SQ. FT.

SECOND FLOOR: 976 SQ. FT.

TOTAL: 2,990 SQ. FT.

BONUS SPACE: 390 SQ. FT.

BEDROOMS: 4

BATHROOMS: 3½

WIDTH: 73' - 9"

DEPTH: 55' - 5"

FOUNDATION: CRAWLSPACE, UNFINISHED BASEMENT .

ORDER ONLINE @ EPLANS.COM

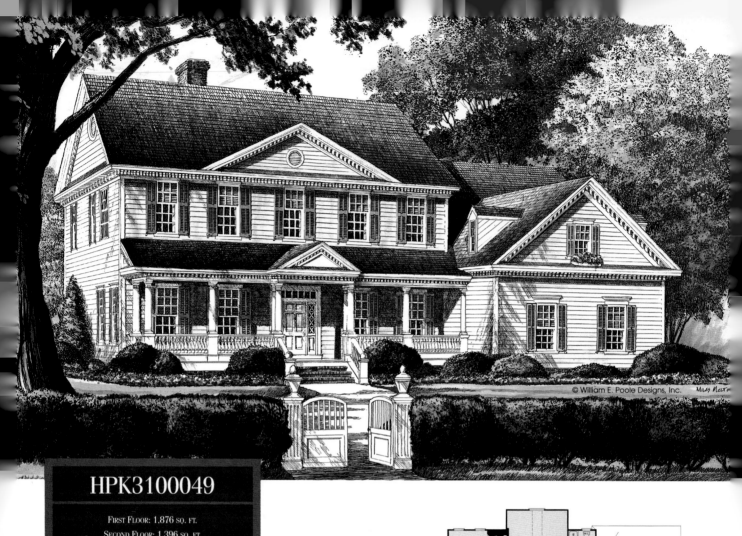

© William E. Poole Designs, Inc. Miles Nelton

HPK3100049

FIRST FLOOR: 1,876 SQ. FT.
SECOND FLOOR: 1,396 SQ. FT.
TOTAL: 3,272 SQ. FT.
BONUS SPACE: 405 SQ. FT.
BEDROOMS: 4
BATHROOMS: 3½
WIDTH: 63' - 4"
DEPTH: 51' - 0"

FOUNDATION: CRAWLSPACE, UNFINISHED BASEMENT

ORDER ONLINE @ EPLANS.COM

Woodbridge

Wandering the back streets of Woodbridge, Connecticut, where we became lost amid all the myriad turns in the roads, we came upon a perfectly proportioned home. The Woodbridge is so intriguing that we looked, admired, walked on, and returned yet again for another admiring glance. With the tolling of the church bells, instant thoughts of being in another era surfaced—thoughts of a simpler time and place.

SECOND FLOOR

FIRST FLOOR

© William E. Poole Designs, Inc.

SECOND FLOOR

FIRST FLOOR

HPK3100051

FIRST FLOOR: 1,904 SQ. FT.

SECOND FLOOR: 1,098 SQ. FT.

TOTAL: 3,002 SQ. FT.

BONUS SPACE: 522 SQ. FT.

BEDROOMS: 4

BATHROOMS: 4½

WIDTH: 88' - 2"

DEPTH: 54' - 0"

FOUNDATION: Crawlspace, Unfinished Basement

ORDER ONLINE @ EPLANS.COM

Hudson Valley II

Having grown up in an old Dutch Colonial out in the country, with wide open spaces, I longed to recreate this charm and quaintness for my city-born brood. I wanted space with warmth, modern conveniences without obvious intrusion, old beams in the ceilings, and a loving, nestled look of belonging. The Hudson Valley II is the home of my dreams--the home where mine shall have dreams of their own.

HPK3100052

First Floor: 1,887 sq. ft.

Second Floor: 1,133 sq. ft.

Total: 3,020 sq. ft.

Bonus Space: 444 sq. ft.

Bedrooms: 4

Bathrooms: 4½

Width: 63' - 4"

Depth: 82' - 2"

Foundation: Crawlspace, Unfinished Basement

ORDER ONLINE @ EPLANS.COM

Baystreet

She grew up in this home. It was here long before she was born. There was no interior stairway then and, no matter the weather or time of day, all ups and downs were by way of the front porch steps. She never questioned the function of Baystreet (it was simply home to her), but her college friends thought it quaint. Today, all renovations are complete, modern amenities discreetly abound, and her children frolic all around—as well as up and down—both staircases, one within and one without.

FIRST FLOOR

SECOND FLOOR

SECOND FLOOR

FIRST FLOOR

HPK3100053

First Floor: 1,973 sq. ft.

Second Floor: 1,062 sq. ft.

Total: 3,035 sq. ft.

Bonus Space: 384 sq. ft.

Bedrooms: 4

Bathrooms: 3½

Width: 57' - 2"

Depth: 60' - 2"

Foundation: Crawlspace, Unfinished Basement

ORDER ONLINE @ EPLANS.COM

Avignon

In the south of France there is an old and ornate town that is filled to the brim with art, beauty, and history. My Wilmington friends, in order to make their travel connections elsewhere, needed to locate the train station in Avignon. They consulted their guidebook, they consulted their language translator, they attempted communication—all to no avail. Finally, Bobby (in utter desperation) approached an elderly man and motioned up and down with his right arm while saying, "Choo-Choo." This was all that was needed for them to finally receive directions to the depot. "C'est la vie!"

Sulphur Springs

The planters' cottage architecture that is so appealing in The Natchez (my most popular home design ever) has now been translated into this smaller, yet perfect new version. There were so many requests for a home in this same character, but with less square footage while maintaining the charm and proportion that—lo and behold, the Sulpher Springs has arrived!

William E. Poole Designs, Inc.

SECOND FLOOR

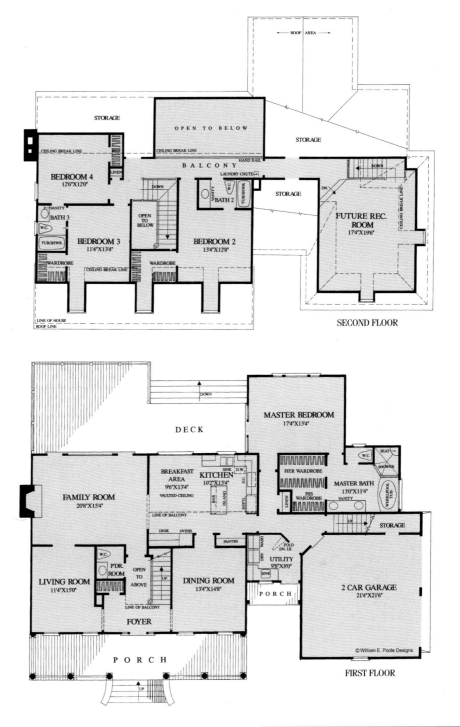

STORAGE

OPEN TO BELOW

STORAGE

BEDROOM 4
12'6"X12'0"

CEILING BREAK LINE

CEILING BREAK LINE

BALCONY

HAND RAIL

STORAGE

LINEN

LAUNDRY CHUTE

DOWN

DOWN

VANITY

W.C.

BATH 3

VANITY

W.C.

BATH 2

TUB/SHWR.

OPEN TO BELOW

FUTURE REC. ROOM
17'4"X19'6"

BEDROOM 3
11'4"X13'4"

BEDROOM 2
13'4"X12'8"

TUB/SHWR.

WARDROBE

CEILING BREAK LINE

WARDROBE

LINE OF HOUSE ROOF LINE

SECOND FLOOR

FIRST FLOOR

DOWN

DECK

MASTER BEDROOM
17'4"X13'4"

BREAKFAST AREA
9'6"X13'4"

VAULTED CEILING

KITCHEN
10'2"X13'4"

SINK

D.W.

STG.

HER WARDROBE

FAMILY ROOM
20'8"X15'4"

BAR

ISLAND

REFG.

W.C.

SEAT

SHOWER

LINEN

HIS WARDROBE

MASTER BATH
13'0"X11'4"

VANITY

WHIRLPOOL TUB

LINE OF BALCONY

DESK

OVENS

PANTRY

DRY.

WASH.

FOLD DN. I.B.

UP

STORAGE

W.C.

PDR. ROOM

OPEN TO ABOVE

UP

DINING ROOM
13'4"X14'8"

UTILITY
9'8"X8'0"

SINK

PORCH

2 CAR GARAGE
21'4"X21'6"

LIVING ROOM
11'4"X15'0"

FOYER

LINE OF BALCONY

© William E. Poole Designs

PORCH

UP

PORCH

FIRST FLOOR

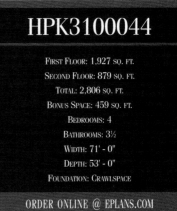

HPK3100044

FIRST FLOOR: 1,927 SQ. FT.
SECOND FLOOR: 879 SQ. FT.
TOTAL: 2,806 SQ. FT.
BONUS SPACE: 459 SQ. FT.
BEDROOMS: 4
BATHROOMS: 3½
WIDTH: 71' - 0"
DEPTH: 53' - 0"
FOUNDATION: CRAWLSPACE

ORDER ONLINE @ EPLANS.COM

Palmetto

There is a very special home that sits on a corner of Meeting Street in Charleston, South Carolina. While being over-shadowed by larger and more grandiose homes, the Palmetto speaks softly, yet takes a back seat to no another. The delicate proportions and simplistic charm of this home purport a simple dignity that captures one's very heart. It's no wonder that all who return can hardly wait to hear the familiar, "welcome home."

PHOTO COURTESY OF WILLIAM E. POOLE DESIGNS, INC. WILMINGTON NC.
THIS HOME, AS SHOWN IN THE PHOTOGRAPH, MAY DIFFER FROM THE ACTUAL BLUEPRINTS. FOR MORE DETAILED INFORMATION, PLEASE CHECK THE FLOOR PLANS CAREFULLY.

SECOND FLOOR

FIRST FLOOR

HPK3100055

FIRST FLOOR: 1,995 SQ. FT.

SECOND FLOOR: 1,062 SQ. FT.

TOTAL: 3,057 SQ. FT.

BONUS SPACE: 459 SQ. FT.

BEDROOMS: 4

BATHROOMS: 3½

WIDTH: 71' - 0"

DEPTH: 57' - 4"

FOUNDATION: UNFINISHED BASEMENT

ORDER ONLINE @ EPLANS.COM

HPK3100056

FIRST FLOOR: 2,357 SQ. FT.

SECOND FLOOR: 772 SQ. FT.

TOTAL: 3,129 SQ. FT.

BONUS SPACE: 450 SQ. FT.

BEDROOMS: 4

BATHROOMS: 3

WIDTH: 69' - 4"

DEPTH: 67' - 4"

FOUNDATION: CRAWLSPACE

ORDER ONLINE @ EPLANS.COM

Mulberry Farm

Miss Helen taught my mother in second grade, taught me in second grade and Sunday school, and was our friend and neighbor. She lived in her old homeplace, and we were always welcomed with a cookie when we dropped in for a visit. Once I came with my first-born, and Miss Helen pulled out some old primers that had my name written on the inside cover. She gave them to my child, and he has them to this day. Many stories abound about Miss Helen, all full of wit and charm and fond memories of her and her homeplace, Mulberry Farm.

SECOND FLOOR

FIRST FLOOR

A pedimented entry and symmetrical facade are marks of the Adams-Federal Colonial influence.

Providence

Look no further for a luxurious design with lasting character

The Adams and Federal homes of Rhode Island and Connecticut were the inspiration for this design. The Providence upholds the Colonial splendor associated with those styles, as do many of the homes in our "Timeless Grandeur" section. Palladian windows, fluted pilasters, and pedimented entries flourish in this section of luxurious dwellings with historical appeal.

A curved staircase greets visitors at the entrance of the Providence. A formal dining room is on the right and a living room with a fireplace is on the left. Continue through the foyer to the family room, where a second fireplace warms on cool nights. During summer months, use the glass doors to directly access a rear deck. Turn to the right for a snack; an island kitchen has plenty of room for casual meals. Turn left to reach the study—which easily functions as a home office—or to relax in the master bedroom. In this private retreat, homeowners can rest easily in a spacious bedroom, or have a spa experience in the bath with double vanities, shower, and whirlpool tub. Endeavor to fill the immense closet space provided by the His and Hers walk-in wardrobe.

Timeless Grandeur

ABOVE: A formal living room at the front of the home can be reserved for special occasions and making great first impressions. RIGHT: A Palladian window graces the wall of this bedroom where a pastel palette complements a garden motif.

Upstairs, children and guests also reap the benefits of this opulent design. Three bedrooms each have their own full bath. One includes a walk-in closet; the remaining two have generous reach-in closets. Down the hall, a future rec room lies above the garage, waiting to be finished and house numerous amusements.

Homes that I have enjoyed in my travels throughout Rhode Island and Connecticut were my inspiration for the Providence.

Timeless Grandeur

Many homes can have a large square footage and plentiful amenities, but few include that mysterious element that makes a house feel like a home. The designs in this section incorporate decades of design elements to achieve that feeling—one of character, history, and "Timeless Grandeur." ■

RIGHT: What a welcome! The foyer greets visitors with a curved staircase and arched pass-throughs to the rooms beyond. The sunburst medallion on the hardwood floor adds a special touch. BELOW: A kitchen island not only provides additional counter space, but it also has extra cabinet storage and can serve as a snack bar for quick meals.

Bold colors in the dining room pleasingly contrast with the neutrals of the foyer and nearby living room.

HPK3100057

First Floor: 2,988 sq. ft.

Second Floor: 1,216 sq. ft.

Total: 4,204 sq. ft.

Bonus Space: 485 sq. ft.

Bedrooms: 4

Bathrooms: 4½ + ½

Width: 83' - 0"

Depth: 70' - 4"

Foundation: Crawlspace, Unfinished Basement

ORDER ONLINE @ EPLANS.COM

FIRST FLOOR

SECOND FLOOR

© William E. Poole Designs, Inc.

HPK3100058

FIRST FLOOR: 1,480 SQ. FT.
SECOND FLOOR: 1,651 SQ. FT.
TOTAL: 3,131 SQ. FT.
BEDROOMS: 4
BATHROOMS: 3½
WIDTH: 67' - 5"
DEPTH: 61' - 5"
FOUNDATION: Crawlspace

ORDER ONLINE @ EPLANS.COM

The Southport

If you have not seen the movie "Crimes of the Heart," you must. The Victorian home refurbished by the set designer on location in Southport, North Carolina, is the inspiration for my rendition. The cupola, the turret, the gazebo, the stained-glass windows, the porches, and the delicate detail all accurately portray the Victorian period, along with a floor plan for today. Welcome home to The Southport.

SECOND FLOOR

FIRST FLOOR

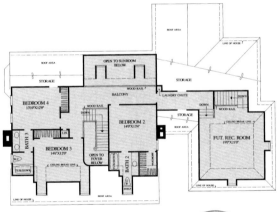

SECOND FLOOR

FIRST FLOOR

HPK3100059

FIRST FLOOR: 2,092 SQ. FT.

SECOND FLOOR: 1,045 SQ. FT.

TOTAL: 3,137 SQ. FT.

BONUS SPACE: 546 SQ. FT.

BEDROOMS: 4

BATHROOMS: 3½

WIDTH: 77' - 0"

DEPTH: 56' - 4"

FOUNDATION: CRAWLSPACE

ORDER ONLINE @ EPLANS.COM

La Petite Natchez

It is often said that good things come in small packages—ask any connoisseur of fine jewelry! You made a request and we listened, thus from The Natchez sprang The La Petite Natchez. Without sacrificing any of the rooms or amenities of the original, The Natchez was proportionately reduced and The La Petite Natchez was born. This generation will create the history for the La Petite. May it be a gracious time!

Rose Hill

Atop a knoll in the historic district of Lexington, Kentucky, sits a lovely southern home, the Rose Hill. The streets all meet and rise to greet this grand old house. Awe is instinctive, yet the closer one gets, the broader one smiles. Children tumble about the yard, pets frolic alongside, and a lemonade stand is set up beside the drive. As one quickly observes, the formality of the home is a deceptive foil for the rollicking family who live within.

GARAGE
21'0"X23'0"

© William E. Poole Designs

TERRACE

STORAGE

WASH DRY UTILITY SINK

PORCH

FAMILY ROOM
18'0"X19'0"
VAULTED TRAY
CEILING

BOOKCASE

MASTER BEDROOM
15'0"X19'0"

SHWR. WHIRLPOOL TUB W.C.

MASTER BATH

LINEN

BEDROOM 4
11'0"X13'0"

BATH 3

TUB/SHWR

BROOM

BREAKFAST
AREA
14'6"X12'0"

ENTERTAINMENT CENTER

WARDROBE

S.U.

OVENS

KITCHEN
16'0"X13'0"

DORIC COLUMNS

SINK

SINK

REFG.

PANTRY DESK

LIVING ROOM
18'6"X13'0"

POWDER ROOM

W.C.

BEDROOM 3
15'6"X13'0"

BEDROOM 2
16'0"X13'8"

DINING ROOM
16'0"X14'0"

FOYER

BATH 2

LINEN

W.C.

TUB/SHWR

PORTICO

HPK3100060

SQUARE FOOTAGE: 3,136

BEDROOMS: 4

BATHROOMS: 3½

WIDTH: 80' - 6"

DEPTH: 72' - 4"

FOUNDATION: CRAWLSPACE

ORDER ONLINE @ EPLANS.COM

Belle Grove

An inviting home, the Belle Grove bespeaks magnolias, dogwood blossoms, butterflies, and the peaceful hospitality of the gracious South. Its inspiration came from Cottage Gardens. A noteworthy feature is the rare combination of the Natchez gallery recessed beneath an unbroken slope of gable roof with a triangular pediment. This home takes its cue from the gracious formality indigenous to the typical Mississippi River Delta planter's cottage.

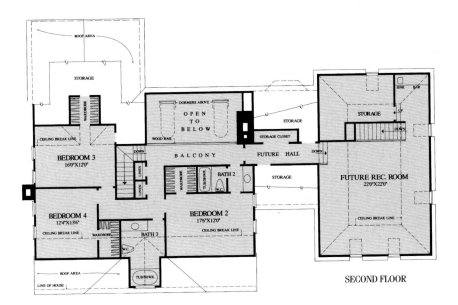

ROOF AREA

STORAGE

CEILING BREAK LINE

BEDROOM 3
16'0"X12'0"

WARDROBE

DOWN

LINEN

LINEN

BEDROOM 4
12'4"X13'6"

CEILING BREAK LINE

WARDROBE

W.C.

BATH 3

W.C.

TUB/SHWR.

ROOF AREA

LINE OF HOUSE

DORMERS ABOVE

OPEN
TO
BELOW

WOOD RAIL

BALCONY

WARDROBE

TUB/SHWR.

BATH 2

W.C.

FUTURE HALL

STORAGE

STORAGE CLOSET

STORAGE

SINK   BAR

STORAGE

DOWN

DOWN

FUTURE REC. ROOM
22'0"X22'0"

CEILING BREAK LINE

BEDROOM 2
17'6"X12'0"

CEILING BREAK LINE

SECOND FLOOR

MASTER BEDROOM
21'0"X14'0"

DECK

STOOP

SHWR.

MASTER
BATH

WHIRLPOOL
TUB

W.C.

LINEN

WARDROBE

LINEN

PDR.
ROOM

W.C.

FAMILY ROOM
21'0"X14'6"

ENTERTAINMENT
CENTER

LINE OF BALCONY

BREAKFAST AREA
12'6"X11'0"

PANTRY

FOLD
DN LR.

DRY   WASH

SINK

UTILITY

STORAGE

UP

LIVING ROOM
16'0"X14'6"

UP

FOYER

DINING ROOM
16'0"X12'6"

KITCHEN
12'10"X12'6"

ISLAND

SINK

OVENS

STU.

REFG.   SINK   D.W.

2 CAR GARAGE
22'0"X22'0"

©William E. Poole Designs

FRONT PORCH

FIRST FLOOR

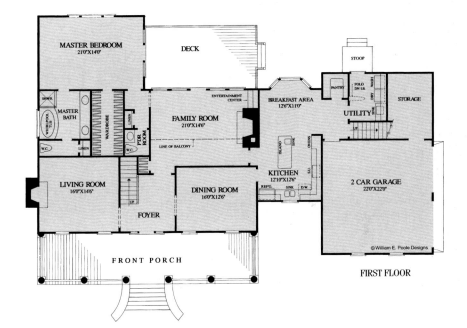

HPK3100061

First Floor: 2,031 sq. ft.
Second Floor: 1,113 sq. ft.
Total: 3,144 sq. ft.
Bonus Space: 683 sq. ft.
Bedrooms: 4
Bathrooms: 3½
Width: 79' - 10"
Depth: 52' - 4"
Foundation: Crawlspace

ORDER ONLINE @ EPLANS.COM

Chesapeake Bay

Ahh ... the "Chesapeake Bay." What memories ... this private old home on Maryland's Eastern shore has gracious lawns spreading beyond the porches all the way to the water's edge. It's the perfect place for gatherings, garden parties, weddings, afternoon teas, croquet, cookouts, and the most tantalizing treat of all—local crabs boiled in spices and served up in buckets as (mallets in hand) one anticipates the noisy, tasty, and fun-filled evening with friends and family.

SECOND FLOOR

- ROOF AREA
- ROOF AREA
- BATH 4 / VANITY / W.C.
- BEDROOM 4 16'8"X12'0"
- BATH 3 / VANITY / W.C. / SHOWER / SEAT
- BATH 2 / VANITY / SHOWER / SEAT
- FUTURE REC ROOM 22'0"X16'4"
- CEILING BREAKLINE
- CEILING BREAK LINE
- WALK IN CLOSET
- HANDRAIL
- LIN
- STOR
- WALK IN CLOSET
- BEDROOM 3 13'0"X16'0"
- OPEN TO BELOW
- BEDROOM 2 13'0"X12'4"
- STORAGE
- DECK

FIRST FLOOR

- MASTER BEDROOM 15'0"X18'0"
- WHIRLPOOL TUB / W.C.
- ENTERTAINMENT CENTER
- BREAKFAST AREA
- OVENS / S.U.
- HIS/HER WARDROBE
- MASTER BATH / VANITY / SHOWER SEAT / LIN
- FAMILY ROOM 24'8"X16'0"
- KITCHEN 12'4"X16'0"
- BAR / SINK / D.W.
- REFRIG
- LIVING ROOM 13'0"X16'0"
- FOYER TWO STORY CEILING 10'4"X12'4"
- DINING ROOM 13'0"X16'0"
- PANTRY
- PDR ROOM / VANITY / W.C.
- UTILITY 12'4"X8'0" / DRIP/DRY / DRY / WASH / SINK
- 2 CAR GARAGE 22'0"X23'0"
- PORCH

©William E. Poole Designs

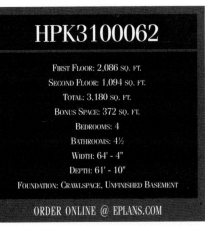

HPK3100062

FIRST FLOOR: 2,086 SQ. FT.
SECOND FLOOR: 1,094 SQ. FT.
TOTAL: 3,180 SQ. FT.
BONUS SPACE: 372 SQ. FT.
BEDROOMS: 4
BATHROOMS: 4½
WIDTH: 64' - 4"
DEPTH: 61' - 10"
FOUNDATION: CRAWLSPACE, UNFINISHED BASEMENT

ORDER ONLINE @ EPLANS.COM

Melrose

Porch swings, trailing wisteria vines, crocuses that look like Easter eggs, buttercups, and chirping birds—all senses are invaded with memories of our childhood. Visits to Grandma's home included stories told, stories heard, and stories embellished. The best possible gift—here we were taught the lessons it had taken our grandparents a lifetime to learn. All this beauty, and a legacy too, was set in the old South—and in the Melrose.

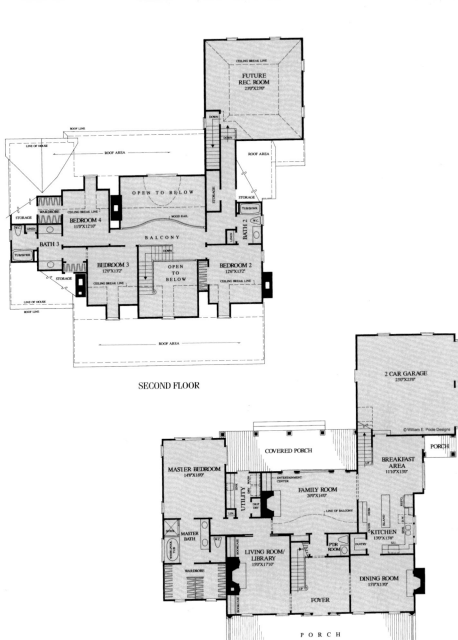

SECOND FLOOR

Second floor labels: FUTURE REC. ROOM 23'0"X23'0", ROOF LINE, LINE OF HOUSE, ROOF AREA, DOWN, STORAGE, WARDROBE, CEILING BREAK LINE, OPEN TO BELOW, WOOD RAIL, BEDROOM 4 11'0"X12'0", BALCONY, STORAGE, W.C., LINEN, BATH 3, TUB/SHWR, BEDROOM 3 12'0"X13'2", STORAGE, OPEN TO BELOW, DOWN, BEDROOM 2 12'6"X13'2", BATH 2, LINEN, TUB/SHWR, W.C., CEILING BREAK LINE, LINE OF HOUSE, ROOF LINE, ROOF AREA

FIRST FLOOR

First floor labels: 2 CAR GARAGE 23'0"X23'0", COVERED PORCH, PORCH, © William E. Poole Designs, BREAKFAST AREA 11'10"X13'0", MASTER BEDROOM 14'8"X18'0", ENTERTAINMENT CENTER, UTILITY, FAMILY ROOM 20'0"X14'0", LINE OF BALCONY, KITCHEN 13'0"X13'8", ISLAND, PANTRY, MASTER BATH, WHIRLPOOL TUB, BOOKCASE, PDR., DESK, LIVING ROOM/LIBRARY 15'0"X17'10", WARDROBE, FOYER, DINING ROOM 15'0"X13'0", PORCH

HPK3100063

FIRST FLOOR: 2,200 SQ. FT.
SECOND FLOOR: 1,001 SQ. FT.
TOTAL: 3,201 SQ. FT.
BONUS SPACE: 674 SQ. FT.
BEDROOMS: 4
BATHROOMS: 3½
WIDTH: 70' - 4"
DEPTH: 74' - 4"
FOUNDATION: CRAWLSPACE

ORDER ONLINE @ EPLANS.COM

HPK3100112

SQUARE FOOTAGE: 2,249
BEDROOMS: 3
BATHROOMS: 2
WIDTH: 72' - 6"
DEPTH: 76' - 8"
FOUNDATION: CRAWLSPACE

ORDER ONLINE @ EPLANS.COM

©1993 William E Poole Designs, Inc

Miz Lossie's House

Whenever I went to Miz Lossie's house there was the wonderful aroma of baking and there was always a special treat "just for me." There were flowers everywhere, both inside and out, and time for a story about "the little green elf" or about her youth, or about the escapades of her children. Miz Lossie had the ability to see beauty in the smallest of things and to create elegance from the least of these. She was a very special person for she was, after all, grandmother.

© William E. Poole Designs, Inc.

SECOND FLOOR

FIRST FLOOR

Saint Clair

All it takes is a smile. This is a truth known everywhere, but we found it especially so in the tiny Normandy village of Saint Clair. Speaking no French other than "bonjour" or "merci," we discovered rather quickly that a word and a smile (coupled with the requisite hand gestures, of course) was all it took for easy understanding. The people of Saint Clair made us feel right at home—"Southern hospitality" at its best.

The Airlie

In a tranquil setting down by the waterway is The Airlie. Weddings in the chapel, festivities on the grounds, and strolls among the gardens are memories to be treasured by more than just a few. Huge live oaks, masses of azaleas in an amazing array of color, and open patches of sun-drenched grassy areas surround this lovely home.

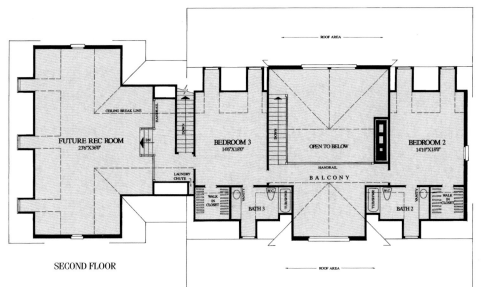

SECOND FLOOR

ROOF AREA

FUTURE REC ROOM
23'6"X36'0"

CEILING BREAK LINE

HANDRAIL

DN

DOWN

DOWN

BEDROOM 3
14'6"X18'0"

OPEN TO BELOW

BEDROOM 2
14'10"X18'0"

HANDRAIL

LAUNDRY CHUTE

B A L C O N Y

WALK IN CLOSET

VANITY

BATH 3

W.C.

TUB/SHWR

TUB/SHWR

W.C.

BATH 2

VANITY

WALK IN CLOSET

ROOF AREA

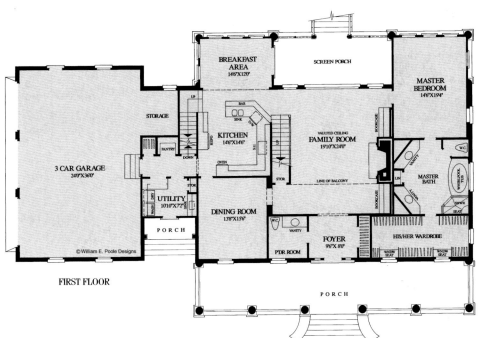

FIRST FLOOR

BREAKFAST AREA
14'6"X12'0"

SCREEN PORCH

STORAGE

UP

MASTER BEDROOM
14'6"X19'4"

3 CAR GARAGE
24'0"X36'0"

PANTRY

DOWN

BAR

SINK

KITCHEN
14'6"X14'6"

RISERS

UP

VAULTED CEILING
FAMILY ROOM
19'10"X24'0"

BOOKCASE

W.C.

OVEN

MASTER BATH

STOR.

LINE OF BALCONY

WHIRLPOOL TUB

UTILITY
10'10"X7'2"

WASH

DRY

SINK

STOR.

DINING ROOM
13'8"X15'6"

BOOKCASE

LIN

LIN

SHWR

SEAT

P O R C H

W.C.

VANITY

P'DR ROOM

FOYER
9'6"X8'0"

HIS/HER WARDROBE

WNDW SEAT

WNDW SEAT

© William E. Poole Designs

P O R C H

© William E. Poole Designs, Inc.

HPK3100066

FIRST FLOOR: 1,978 SQ. FT.

SECOND FLOOR: 1,320 SQ. FT.

TOTAL: 3,298 SQ. FT.

BONUS SPACE: 352 SQ. FT.

BEDROOMS: 4

BATHROOMS: 3½

WIDTH: 66' - 8"

DEPTH: 62' - 0"

FOUNDATION: CRAWLSPACE

ORDER ONLINE @ EPLANS.COM

River Road

High above the Suwannee River sits an old Southern plantation home replete with Spanish moss swaying in the gentle breezes and bougainvillea vines exploding with color. I remembered similar warm evenings when my father would take us to get a block of ice so we could make cream. With fireflies dancing, stories entrancing, swinging soothing, and ice cream cooling—what a blissful way to end a day both then and now, down home at River Road.

SECOND FLOOR

FIRST FLOOR

© William E. Poole Designs, Inc.

SECOND FLOOR

FIRST FLOOR

HPK3100067

FIRST FLOOR: 2,320 SQ. FT.

SECOND FLOOR: 1,009 SQ. FT.

TOTAL: 3,329 SQ. FT.

BONUS SPACE: 521 SQ. FT.

BEDROOMS: 4

BATHROOMS: 3½

WIDTH: 80' - 4"

DEPTH: 58' - 0"

FOUNDATION: CRAWLSPACE

ORDER ONLINE @ EPLANS.COM

St. Charles

New Orleans, famous for the French Quarter with its Dixieland jazz, Creole delights, and beignets, is an exhilarating experience. In contrast, the quiet Garden District with the streetcar ride to Audubon Park, ancient trees lining the avenues, and gracious homes along the way, are pure delight. Listen and you can hear hooves beating along the paths, children laughing at play, and violins as the waltz begins—all from times past. The St. Charles is reminiscent of there and then, but is a home for here and now.

HELPFUL HINT! A Smart House design enables universal control of home theater, security, and audio systems.

Philadelphia

Our Liberty Bell, Ben Franklin's print shop, the signing of the Declaration of Independence—what history one feels
in the streets of Philadelphia. So many beginnings and so many endings in the foundation and growth of our country
have their roots in this city. Classical and commanding, the Philadelphia is typical of many homes in the Historic
District and would be majestic in any neighborhood anywhere—today as well as yesterday and tomorrow.

FUTURE REC. ROOM
16'2"X23'0"

STORAGE

DOWN

STORAGE

ROOF AREA

ROOF AREA

STOR.

OPEN TO BELOW

BEDROOM 4
13'6"X12'8"

OPTIONAL
BEDROOM 5
15'8"X13'2"

BALCONY
HANDRAIL

STORAGE

VANITY

W.C.

BATH 2
TUB/SHWR

HANDRAIL

DOWN

TUB/SHWR

W.C.

BATH 3

VANITY

BEDROOM 2
13'4"X14'4"

OPEN TO BELOW

BEDROOM 3
13'4"X12'4"

ROOF AREA

WALK IN CLOSET

WINDOW SEAT

SECOND FLOOR

2 CAR GARAGE
22'0"X23'0"

© William E. Poole Designs

STORAGE

REAR ENTRY

DRIP/DRY

PORCH

FOLD DN. LB.

UTILITY
12'0"X6'8"

DRY   WASH

SINK

ENTERTAINMENT CENTER

FAMILY ROOM
TWO STORY CEILING
20'4"X15'0"

OVENS

S.U.

MASTER BEDROOM
15'8"X15'0"

SINK

ISLAND

BAR

KITCHEN
16'4"X12'0"

REFRIG.

LINE OF BALCONY

WHIRLPOOL

MASTER BATH

LINEN

VANITY

SHOWER SEAT

HIS/HER WARDROBE

WET BAR

SINK

PDR. ROOM

W.C.

DOWN TO BASEMENT

UP

DISK

PANTRY

BREAKFAST AREA
11'9"X9'4"

LIVING ROOM
13'0"X15'8"

FOYER
TWO STORY CEILING
9'4"X15'8"

DINING ROOM
13'4"X12'4"

W.C.

FIRST FLOOR

Greenville

As all-American as apple pie, baseball, and Norman Rockwell paintings—the Greenville is a classic. You have the desire, why not have the dream—the American dream of having your very own home on a pleasant, tree-lined street where children play, neighbors visit, church bells ring, and lasting friendships are made.

SECOND FLOOR

ROOF AREA

STORAGE

OPEN TO BELOW

ROOF AREA

CEILING BREAK LINE

FUTURE REC. ROOM
18'4"X16'8"

STORAGE

HANDRAIL

BALCONY

HANDRAIL

DOWN

TUB/SHWR

LAV.

W.C.

BATH 3

BEDROOM 4
15'4"X12'0"

STORAGE

CEILING BREAK LINE

ROOF AREA

ROOF AREA

FIRST FLOOR

BREAKFAST AREA
12'0"X12'0"

DESK

BEDROOM 2
13'10"X13'0"

FAMILY ROOM
20'0"X21'10"

VOLUME CEILING

BAR

MASTER BEDROOM
17'0"X15'0"

BOOKCASE

SINK

D.W

KITCHEN
14'0"X12'8"

REF'G

BOOKCASE

S.U.

W.C.

WHIRLPOOL TUB/SHOWER

LINEN

BATH 2

OVENS

PANTRY

LINEN

LAV.

SEAT

SHOWER

LINE OF BALCONY

LAV.

BEDROOM 3
12'0"X15'6"

P'DR ROOM

LAV.

UP TO FUTURE SECOND FLOOR

CLOS

W.C.

DRIP DRY

MASTER BATH

WHIRLPOOL TUB

LIVING ROOM
13'0"X20'2"

FOYER

DINING ROOM
15'0"X12'0"

WASH

SHLVS

HIS WARDROBE

SHLVS

HER WARDROBE

W.C.

DRY

UTILITY

SINK

PORCH

2 CAR GARAGE
21'0"X23'0"

© William E. Poole Designs

STORAGE

ns, Inc.

HPK3100069

FIRST FLOOR: 2,818 SQ. FT.

SECOND FLOOR: 533 SQ. FT.

TOTAL: 3,351 SQ. FT.

BONUS SPACE: 323 SQ. FT.

BEDROOMS: 4

BATHROOMS: 3½

WIDTH: 69' - 0"

DEPTH: 70' - 11"

FOUNDATION: CRAWLSPACE

ORDER ONLINE @ EPLANS.COM

© William E. Poole Designs, Inc.

HPK3100070

First Floor: 2,337 sq. ft.

Second Floor: 1,016 sq. ft.

Total: 3,353 sq. ft.

Bonus Space: 394 sq. ft.

Bedrooms: 4

Bathrooms: 3½

Width: 66' - 2"

Depth: 71' - 2"

Foundation: Crawlspace

ORDER ONLINE @ EPLANS.COM

The Shields Town House

We were looking for the perfect home. It had to be charming and cozy, classical in proportion, and timeless in design—not too big and not too little. It had to be just right, and above all, it had to be built of brick. One house rambled, one was too formal, and all were wrong for us in one way or another until suddenly we saw it—The Shields Town House in Natchez, Mississippi—the home of our dreams.

SECOND FLOOR

FIRST FLOOR

© William E. Poole Designs, Inc.

SECOND FLOOR

FIRST FLOOR

HPK3100071

First Floor: 2,099 sq. ft.

Second Floor: 1,260 sq. ft.

Total: 3,359 sq. ft.

Bonus Space: 494 sq. ft.

Bedrooms: 4

Bathrooms: 3½

Width: 68' - 4"

Depth: 54' - 0"

Foundation: Crawlspace

ORDER ONLINE @ EPLANS.COM

Saratoga Springs

Ahhh ... the memory of a crisp August morning filled with brilliant color and constrained excitement as we walked with myriad others along the tree-lined streets toward the racetrack. The homes along the way were radiant with flowers and festivities. A Victorian avenue from another era, it seemed, come to life for the annual Travers Stakes once again—down home in Saratoga Springs.

© William E. Poole D

The Hamilton

"Quality versus quantity." This guiding rule was not only drilled into my head growing up but, in my maturing years, observed and acknowledged as a wise and lasting truth. Details make all the difference, and in homes they are the defining difference that sometimes dictates less in square footage in order to complete our total vision—details that enhance and solidify our home for the memories we make. The Hamilton typifies the translation from grand estate to the human scale and is more than worthy of this old adage.

SECOND FLOOR

WARDROBE

BEDROOM 3
16'-4"X12'-2"

BATH 3

BATH 2

BATH 4

LINEN

STORAGE

FUTURE
REC. ROOM
19'-10" X 19'-8"

9'-4" CEILING
BREAKLINE

ROOF AREA

HANDRAIL

DOWN

UP

9'-0" CEILING BREAKLINE

HANDRAIL

DOWN

BEDROOM 2
13'-0"X15'-6"

BEDROOM 4
13'-0"X12'-4"

OPEN TO
BELOW

WARDROBE

WARDROBE

STORAGE

ROOF AREA

ROOF AREA

STORAGE

STORAGE

FIRST FLOOR

MASTER
BEDROOM
15'-0"X18'-0"

WHIRLPOOL
TUB

MASTER
BATH

WARDROBE

LINEN

BREAKFAST
AREA
10'-4" X 12'-0"

OVENS   S. U.

DW

FAMILY ROOM
22'-0"X16'-0"

BAR   ISLAND

KITCHEN
13'-0"X16'-0"

REFG.

BOOKCASE

LIVING
ROOM
13'-0"X16'-0"

FOYER
10'-4"X12'-4"
2 STORY CEILING

UP

DINING
ROOM
13'-0"X16'-0"

PANTRY

UTILITY

SINK

D.

W.

POWDER
ROOM

DOWN

STORAGE

2 CAR GARAGE
22'-0"X23'-0"

PORCH

© William E. Poole Designs

ns, Inc.

Miles Melton

HPK3100072

FIRST FLOOR: 2,168 SQ. FT.

SECOND FLOOR: 1,203 SQ. FT.

TOTAL: 3,371 SQ. FT.

BONUS SPACE: 452 SQ. FT.

BEDROOMS: 4

BATHROOMS: 4½

WIDTH: 71' - 2"

DEPTH: 63' - 4"

FOUNDATION: CRAWLSPACE, UNFINISHED BASEMENT

ORDER ONLINE @ EPLANS.COM

Sunnyside

Fine china and milk-laced tea, melt-in-your-mouth shortbread cookies, and cocoa-dusted meringues—for two little girls dressed in their Sunday best—this was the epitome of elegance. Our weekly afternoon tea with Grammie was a ritual never missed. Sunnyside—her tidewater Virginian farmhouse—is a quietly elegant home with a warm, welcoming porch that invites tea parties and other lasting traditions.

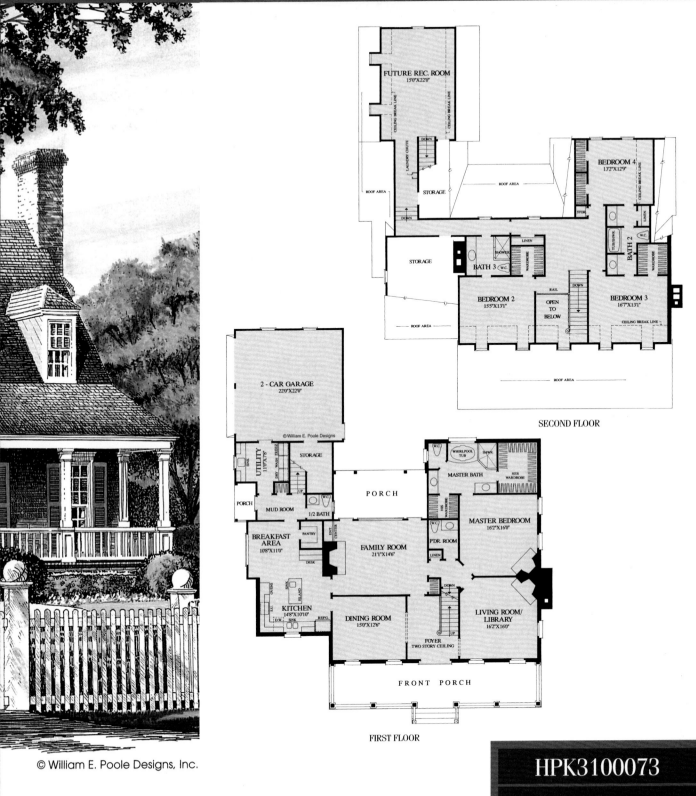

FUTURE REC. ROOM
15'0"X22'0"

LAUNDRY CHUTE

DOWN

ROOF AREA

STORAGE

DOWN

ROOF AREA

BEDROOM 4
13'2"X12'9"

STOR.

LINEN

BATH 2

W.C.

TUB/SHWR.

WARDROBE

STORAGE

BATH 3

SHOWER

LINEN

WARDROBE

W.C.

BEDROOM 2
15'5"X13'1"

RAIL

OPEN
TO
BELOW

DOWN

BEDROOM 3
16'7"X13'1"

CEILING BREAK LINE

ROOF AREA

ROOF AREA

SECOND FLOOR

2 - CAR GARAGE
22'0"X22'0"

© William E. Poole Designs

WHIRLPOOL
TUB

W.C.

SHWR.

SINK

UTILITY
11'1"X7'8"

DRY

WASH

FREZ.

STORAGE

PORCH

MUD ROOM

W.C.

1/2 BATH

PORCH

MASTER BATH

HER
WARDROBE

HIS
WARDROBE

MASTER BEDROOM
16'2"X16'0"

BREAKFAST
AREA
10'8"X11'0"

PANTRY

ENT.
CENTER

FAMILY ROOM
21'1"X14'6"

W.C.

PDR. ROOM

LINEN

DESK

KITCHEN
14'8"X10'10"

OVENS

SINK

ISLAND

D.W.

SINK

REFG.

DINING ROOM
15'0"X12'6"

DOWN

UP

FOYER
TWO STORY CEILING

LIVING ROOM/
LIBRARY
16'2"X16'0"

UP

FRONT PORCH

FIRST FLOOR

© William E. Poole Designs, Inc.

HPK3100073

First Floor: 2,193 sq. ft.

Second Floor: 1,179 sq. ft.

Total: 3,372 sq. ft.

Bonus Space: 558 sq. ft.

Bedrooms: 4

Bathrooms: 3½ + ½

Width: 66' - 5"

Depth: 75' - 5"

Foundation: Crawlspace

ORDER ONLINE @ EPLANS.COM

Camellia Cottage II

The struggle to return home. A young girl stands with a wicker basket over one arm while clutching her small dog in the other. She closes her eyes, clicks together the heels of her ruby-red slippers, and utters repeatedly, "There's no place like home." Dorothy, and a multitude of others have touched our hearts and souls with their determination to reach their homes and families. Home. It's more that just a place to live. The Camellia Cottage II is dedicated to the wonderful characters, fictional and nonfictional, that believe home is an essential part of their beings.

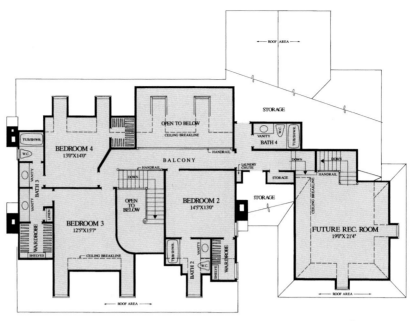

SECOND FLOOR

BEDROOM 4
13'0"X14'0"

OPEN TO BELOW
CEILING BREAKLINE

STORAGE

BATH 3

W.C.

VANITY

VANITY

BALCONY

HANDRAIL

VANITY
BATH 4

W.C.

TUB/SHWR.

WARDROBE

SHELVES

BEDROOM 3
12'5"X15'7"

OPEN TO BELOW

DOWN

HANDRAIL

BEDROOM 2
14'5"X13'0"

LAUNDRY CHUTE

STORAGE

DOWN

DOWN

HANDRAIL

CEILING BREAKLINE

STORAGE

FUTURE REC. ROOM
19'0"X 21'4"

CEILING BREAKLINE

TUB/SHWR.

VANITY

BATH 2

W.C.

WARDROBE

SHELVES

ROOF AREA

ROOF AREA

FIRST FLOOR

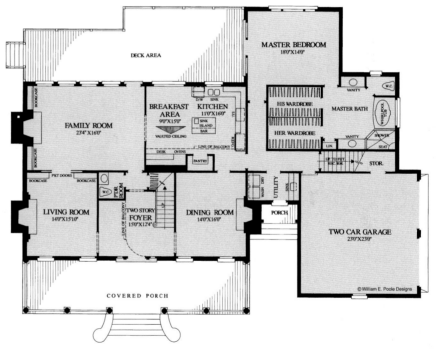

DECK AREA

MASTER BEDROOM
18'0"X14'0"

W.C.

VANITY

BOOKCASE

FAMILY ROOM
23'4"X16'0"

BREAKFAST AREA
9'0"X15'0"

KITCHEN
11'0"X16'0"

D/W SINK

SINK ISLAND

BAR

VAULTED CEILING

HIS WARDROBE

HER WARDROBE

MASTER BATH

WHIRLPOOL TUB

SHOWER

SEAT

LIN.

VANITY

BOOKCASE

DESK OVENS

LINE OF BALCONY

PANTRY

UP TO FUT. REC RM.

STOR.

BOOKCASE

PKT DOORS

BOOKCASE

W.C.

PDR. ROOM

TWO STORY FOYER
15'0"X12'4"

LINE OF BALCONY

DINING ROOM
14'0"X16'0"

PORCH

UTILITY

WASH DRY

SINK

TWO CAR GARAGE
23'0"X23'0"

LIVING ROOM
14'0"X15'10"

© William E. Poole Designs

COVERED PORCH

HPK3100074

FIRST FLOOR: 2,320 SQ. FT.

SECOND FLOOR: 1,057 SQ. FT.

TOTAL: 3,377 SQ. FT.

BONUS SPACE: 608 SQ. FT.

BEDROOMS: 4

BATHROOMS: 4½

WIDTH: 81' - 4"

DEPTH: 58' - 2"

FOUNDATION: CRAWLSPACE

ORDER ONLINE @ EPLANS.COM

Saint Remy

This elegant and tasteful, yet modest chateau is an exquisite rendition of French Country that stands alone in both character and design. The French people, the land, the architecture, and the cuisine come together in a harmony that exists so perfectly—perhaps nowhere else. The tranquil and natural approach to blending all that is indigenous to the land with thoughtful detail and a heartiness that is so satisfying to all the senses is uniquely Southern—in this case, the wine region of southern France.

ROOF AREA   ROOF AREA   ROOF AREA

CEILING BREAKLINE   DOWN

FUTURE REC. ROOM
17'8"X22'4"

STORAGE

MASTER BEDROOM # 2
18'0"X15'4"

SEAT
SHOWER   WHIRLPOOL TUB   W.C.

MASTER BATH #2
VANITY   LIN.

HIS/HER WARDROBE   SHELV

DOWN   WALK IN CLOSET

SHELV   WALK IN CLOSET

BEDROOM 4
12'0"X12'0"   VANITY   TUB/SHWR   BEDROOM 3
13'0"X12'0"

W.C.   BATH 3   LIN.

ROOF AREA

STORAGE   RAILING

ROOF AREA

STORAGE

SECOND FLOOR

W.C.   SEAT
WHIRLPOOL TUB   SHOWER

MASTER BEDROOM
18'0"X15'0"
VOLUME CEILING

BREAKFAST AREA
13'0"X11'0"   PORCH

MASTER BATH   VANITY   LIN.

UP TO FUTURE REC. ROOM

FAMILY ROOM
20'4"X15'0"

HIS/HER WARDROBE   SHELV   W.C.   VANITY

BAR   D/W   SINK

DRIP DRY   PDR ROOM

KITCHEN
13'0"X13'8"   REF/D.

STORAGE   WASH   DRY   SINK

UTILITY   MUD ROOM   PANTRY   OVENS

UP

PORCH   DINING ROOM
13'0"X13'8"   FOYER
7'6"X11'0"   LIVING ROOM
13'0"X12'0"

2 CAR GARAGE
22'0"X23'0"

© William E. Poole Designs   STOOP

FIRST FLOOR

HPK3100075

FIRST FLOOR: 2,216 SQ. FT.

SECOND FLOOR: 1,192 SQ. FT.

TOTAL: 3,408 SQ. FT.

BONUS SPACE: 458 SQ. FT.

BEDROOMS: 4

BATHROOMS: 3½

WIDTH: 67' - 10"

DEPTH: 56' - 10"

FOUNDATION: CRAWLSPACE

ORDER ONLINE @ EPLANS.COM

Biloxi

All along the Gulf Coast highway, one cannot help but admire the beautiful homes that seemingly go on forever. Shingled cottages (with columned porches sitting amid flowing lawns with large shade trees) hold out an inviting hand to come and dream your dreams right there—in a large old rocking chair with a cool glass of lemonade and an unending view of the sea. Neighbors are friendly, visitors are welcome, "ma'am" and "sir" are the norm, and life is good—as it should be, at home in the Biloxi.

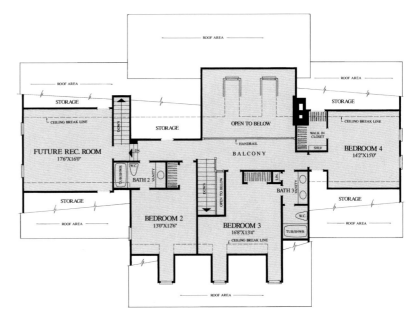

SECOND FLOOR

Second Floor labels

ROOF AREA

ROOF AREA

STORAGE

ROOF AREA

STORAGE

CEILING BREAK LINE

STORAGE

OPEN TO BELOW

WALK IN CLOSET

CEILING BREAK LINE

FUTURE REC. ROOM
17'6"X16'0"

DN.

HANDRAIL

BALCONY

SHLV

BEDROOM 4
14'2"X15'0"

TUB/SHWR

BATH 2

VANITY

DOWN

OPEN TO BELOW

LIN.

BATH 3

VANITY

STORAGE

STORAGE

W.C.

STORAGE

ROOF AREA

BEDROOM 2
13'0"X12'6"

DOWN

BEDROOM 3
16'8"X13'4"

TUB/SHWR

ROOF AREA

CEILING BREAK LINE

ROOF AREA

FIRST FLOOR

First Floor labels

BREAKFAST AREA
VAULTED CEILING
14'0"X12'0"

PORCH
VAULTED CEILING

STOOP

UTILITY
7'6"X9'0"

MUD ROOM

KITCHEN
14'0"X11'8"

ENTERTAINMENT CENTER

STORAGE

WASH DRY

SINK DRY

FOLD DRY

DRIP DRY

UP TO 6'-0 HIGH REC ROOM

BAR

SU

FAMILY ROOM
VAULTED CEILING
21'0"X15'6"

MASTER BEDROOM
18'0"X14'0"

OVENS

SINK

D/W

BAR

CHINA

REFG.

2 CAR GARAGE
21'0"X22'0"

PANTRY

W.C.

VANITY

P'DR ROOM

LINE OF BALCONY

BOOKCASE

W.C.

SEAT SHOWER

LINEN

VANITY

WHIRLPOOL TUB

MASTER BATH

© William E. Poole Designs

UP

GALLERY
24'10"X4'2"

DINING ROOM
13'0"X16'0"

LIVING ROOM
13'0"X16'0"

HIS/HER WARDROBE

FOYER

PORCH

HPK3100076

FIRST FLOOR: 2,191 SQ. FT.

SECOND FLOOR: 1,220 SQ. FT.

TOTAL: 3,411 SQ. FT.

BONUS SPACE: 280 SQ. FT.

BEDROOMS: 4

BATHROOMS: 3½

WIDTH: 75' - 8"

DEPTH: 54' - 4"

FOUNDATION: CRAWLSPACE, UNFINISHED BASEMENT

ORDER ONLINE @ EPLANS.COM

Le Mans

The door opened and we were greeted by a most gracious and lovely lady, the owner of Le Mans. Indeed, her family had lived here for generations and it was only recently that she began using the first floor to display and sell her antiques—exquisite and elegant pieces—each a treasure, much like the home itself. A memory not to be forgotten, but enjoyed for now and always.

William E. Poole Designs, Inc.

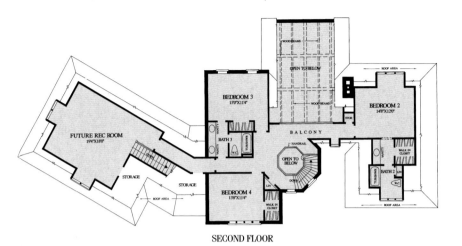

BEDROOM 3
15'0"X11'4"

BATH 3

FUTURE REC ROOM
19'4"X18'0"

STORAGE

STORAGE

ROOF AREA

BEDROOM 4
13'8"X11'4"

WALK IN
CLOSET

OPEN TO BELOW

WOOD BEAMS

WOOD BEAMS

BALCONY

OPEN TO
BELOW

HANDRAIL

DOWN

STOR.

ROOF AREA

BEDROOM 2
14'8"X12'0"

WALK IN
CLOSET

BATH 2

W.C.

ROOF AREA

SECOND FLOOR

WOOD TRELLIS

T E R R A C E

DINING ROOM
15'0"X14'0"

© William E. Poole Designs

2 CAR GARAGE
24'0"X24'0"

STORAGE

UTILITY

PANTRY

KITCHEN
13'8"X11'0"

ISLAND

WOOD BEAMS

PORCH

BREAKFAST
AREA
13'6"X10'0"

PDR
ROOM

W.C.

OPEN TO ABOVE

CATHEDRAL CEILING
GREAT ROOM
18'6"X26'0"

BOOKCASE

ARCHED OPENING

BOOKCASE

FOYER
13'6"X13'0"

STOOP

MASTER BEDROOM
18'0"X17'0"

W.C.

MASTER
BATH

VANITY

VANITY

HIS/HER WARDROBE

FIRST FLOOR

New Iberia

One balmy spring, eight of us, all with Southern roots and a love of things worn well with time, went south—both to enjoy the company and reconnect with our romantic past. And reconnect we did—Cajun music, crayfish gumbo, and boat rides in the bayous were fun alright. However, the most inspiring moment occurred on the upper porch of a grand old home. From there we could hear footsteps on the heart pine floors within, we could see the rolling river beyond the fields below, we could remember the families whose lives made history before our time. This place (New Iberia), this moment—a reflection, a connection with then and now.

SECOND FLOOR

MASTER BATH
KNEE SPACE
WARDROBE
BEDROOM 2
13'-0" X 14'-8"
WALK IN CLOSET
BATH 3
STORAGE
HANDRAIL
DOWN
FUTURE REC. ROOM
20'-10" X 15'-10"
9' CEILING BREAKLINE
DOWN
MASTER BEDROOM
14'-0" X 19'-0"
OPEN TO BELOW
HANDRAIL
LINEN
BEDROOM 3
14'-0" X 12'-4"
UP TO ATTIC
UPPER FOYER
ROOF AREA
ROOF AREA
PORCH
44'-6" X 8'-0"

FIRST FLOOR

TERRACE AREA
2 CAR GARAGE
22'-10" X 23'-0"
© William E. Poole Designs
BOOK CASE
BREAKFAST
9'-0" X 13'-0"
REF'G.
SINK
STORAGE
WASH DRY
SINK
UTILITY
FAMILY ROOM
20'-8" X 14'-8"
SINK
BAR
DESK
KITCHEN
10'-8" X 16'-2"
OVENS
D.W.
STOOP
STOR.
UP
BOOK CASE
P'DR. ROOM
PANTRY
CHINA
REAR ENTRY
PORCH
LIVING ROOM
14'-0" X 15'-10"
LINE OF BALCONY
FOYER
14'-0" X 12'-4"
UP
DINING ROOM
14'-0" X 14'-6"
STORAGE
BATH 2
LIN.
STUDY
13'-0" X 12'-0"
PORCH
44'-6" X 8'-0"

HPK3100078

First Floor: 2,033 sq. ft.

Second Floor: 1,447 sq. ft.

Total: 3,480 sq. ft.

Bonus Space: 411 sq. ft.

Bedrooms: 3

Bathrooms: 3½

Width: 67' - 10"

Depth: 64' - 4"

Foundation: Crawlspace, Unfinished Basement

ORDER ONLINE @ EPLANS.COM

© William E. Poole Designs, Inc.

HPK3100079

First Floor: 2,359 sq. ft.

Second Floor: 1,112 sq. ft.

Total: 3,471 sq. ft.

Bonus Space: 559 sq. ft.

Bedrooms: 4

Bathrooms: 3½

Width: 81' - 8"

Depth: 77' - 8"

Foundation: Crawlspace

ORDER ONLINE @ EPLANS.COM

The Wedge Plantation

Collaboration with a friendly fellow developing Kilgore Plantation in Greenville, South Carolina, resulted in my designing The Wedge Plantation. We determined that a South Carolina historical home should be replicated without but designed within to meet the needs of today. The "original" Wedge, a rice planter's home, possesses a simple, elegant, classical grace with perfect symmetry enhanced by balanced wings. Researching this 1826 plantation home and designing the "new" Wedge has been an enjoyable experience and one that I wish to share with you.

FIRST FLOOR

SECOND FLOOR

SECOND FLOOR

ROOF AREA

OPEN TO BELOW

SKYLIGHT BY OWNER   SKYLIGHT BY OWNER

ROOF AREA

PLANT SHELF

WOOD HANDRAIL

PLANT SHELF (BELOW)

BATH CEILING JOISTS (BELOW)   MASTER SUITE (BELOW)

LOFT
12'-8" X 8'-6"

DOWN

WOOD HANDRAIL

FUTURE REC. ROOM
16'-8" X 13'-0"

9' CEILING BREAKLINE

WALK-IN CLOSET

BEDROOM 2
10'-6" X 12'-6"

BATH 2

BEDROOM 3
11'-8" X 10'-6"

ACCESS DOOR

ATTIC STORAGE

ROOF AREA   ROOF AREA   ROOF AREA

FIRST FLOOR

DECK

BREAKFAST
12'-8" X 10'-8"

VAULT

BAR

LINE OF PLANT SHELF ABOVE

FAMILY ROOM
15'-0" X 14'-4"

VAULT   VAULT   VAULT

GARDEN TUB

MASTER SUITE
13'-4" X 16'-6"

BATH

DW.

LINE OF BALCONY ABOVE

UP

1/2 BATH

SINK

KITCHEN
10'-2" X11'-8"

RANGE

WALK-IN CLOSET

DINING ROOM
10'-6" X 13'-6"

LIVING ROOM
12'-4" X14'-0"

FOYER
4'-8"X 14'-0"

UTILITY

STORAGE
14'-8" X 4'-6"

GAZEBO

PORCH

2 CAR GARAGE
21'-0" X 21'-8"

©William E. Poole Designs

HPK3100080

First Floor: 1,492 sq. ft.
Second Floor: 607 sq. ft.
Total: 2,099 sq. ft.
Bedrooms: 3
Bathrooms: 2½
Width: 61' - 2"
Depth: 58' - 4"
Foundation: Crawlspace

ORDER ONLINE @ EPLANS.COM

Folk Victorian Cottage

Delicate gingerbread details embellish the inviting porches of this gracious Queen Anne home. A formal yet open floor plan makes entertaining a thrill; at the front of the home the living room flows right into the dining room for special occasions; while beyond the staircase, an airy arrangement of skylit family room, vaulted breakfast nook, and spacious kitchen can accomodate more casual family gatherings and everyday activities. The master suite hides in a secluded corner of the main level. Upstairs, two family bedrooms share a bath and a loft area for reading and studying.

© William E. Poole Designs, Inc.

HPK3100082

First Floor: 2,449 sq. ft.

Second Floor: 1,094 sq. ft.

Total: 3,543 sq. ft.

Bonus Space: 409 sq. ft.

Bedrooms: 4

Bathrooms: 3½

Width: 89' - 0"

Depth: 53' - 10"

Foundation: Crawlspace

ORDER ONLINE @ EPLANS.COM

SECOND FLOOR

FIRST FLOOR

Summer Hill

With both pride and affection you watch your bride's reaction when, for the first time, she sees the Summer Hill. Much of who you are has been defined from growing up in this old Greek Revival Virginia plantation house—this wonderful classical home with flair. The wide, meandering porch that can be accessed from all rooms through French doors, the softness of its outline nestled against the trees, the knowledge that the nearby neighborhood sprang up around this romantic but ceremonious home gives you but a moment's pause before hearing her gently say, "How absolutely lovely."

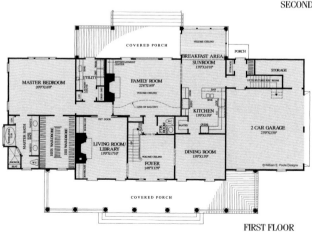

SECOND FLOOR

FIRST FLOOR

HPK3100081

First Floor: 2,568 sq. ft.

Second Floor: 981 sq. ft.

Total: 3,549 sq. ft.

Bedrooms: 4

Bathrooms: 4½

Width: 66' - 8"

Depth: 71' - 0"

Foundation: Unfinished Basement

ORDER ONLINE @ EPLANS.COM

The Thistlewood

If fairy tales are to be believed, and of course they are, then The Thistlewood captures imaginations of romance and brings memories of delightful cottages and their stories to mind—"Goldilocks and the Three Bears," "Little Red Riding Hood," "Snow White and the Seven Dwarfs," and "Jack and the Beanstalk" to name a few. The romance. The charm. The detail. What a delightful home—The Thistlewood.

HPK3100084

FIRST FLOOR: 2,064 SQ. FT.

SECOND FLOOR: 1,521 SQ. FT.

TOTAL: 3,585 SQ. FT.

BONUS SPACE: 427 SQ. FT.

BEDROOMS: 4

BATHROOMS: 3

WIDTH: 84' - 8"

DEPTH: 65' - 0"

FOUNDATION: CRAWLSPACE

ORDER ONLINE @ EPLANS.COM

FIRST FLOOR

SECOND FLOOR

The Josiah Smith House

Would you believe that in the early days of building townhouses in Charleston, South Carolina, brick was more economical (to say nothing of being more fireproof) than wood? As the story goes, when The Josiah Smith House was constructed, the owner resisted all the enticing wiles of his wife and did the embarassing, socially incorrect thing by building his home of brick. As usual, she had the last say. Upon his untimely death, his fortune was put to good use in framing over the entire structure with costly lumber. Whoever said "women always get their way" certainly knew what they were talking about. There must be a moral to this story—somewhere.

HELPFUL HINT! | A materials list outlines your home's building materials, simplifying your cost-to-build estimate.

© William E. Poole Designs, Inc.

HPK3100087

SQUARE FOOTAGE: 3,600
BEDROOMS: 4
BATHROOMS: 3½
WIDTH: 76' - 2"
DEPTH: 100' - 10"
FOUNDATION: CRAWLSPACE, UNFINISHED BASEMENT

ORDER ONLINE @ EPLANS.COM

Mount Ellen

My grandmother wanted everything perfect. She wanted formality with graciousness, comfort with good taste, and most of all, livability with a sense of grandness; but all on a scale that would promote warmth and on a level that would enable her to avoid stairs. My grandmother found perfection with the Mount Ellen, and created her own perfect world within.

MILES MEL

HPK3100083

First Floor: 2,273 sq. ft.

Second Floor: 1,391 sq. ft.

Total: 3,664 sq. ft.

Bonus Space: 547 sq. ft.

Bedrooms: 4

Bathrooms: 4½

Width: 77' - 2"

Depth: 48' - 0"

Foundation: Crawlspace

ORDER ONLINE @ EPLANS.COM

SECOND FLOOR

FIRST FLOOR

Boothe House

An easy and charming interpretation of the late Georgian style, our version, the Boothe House, is carefully adapted to meet the practical requirements of a modern lifestyle. Cased openings, high ceilings, and well-placed windows keep the expansive, comfortable interiors light and open.

SECOND FLOOR

FIRST FLOOR

HPK3100089

FIRST FLOOR: 2,327 SQ. FT.
SECOND FLOOR: 1,431 SQ. FT.
TOTAL: 3,758 SQ. FT.
BONUS SPACE: 473 SQ. FT.
BEDROOMS: 5
BATHROOMS: 3½
WIDTH: 78' - 10"
DEPTH: 58' - 2"
FOUNDATION: CRAWLSPACE, UNFINISHED BASEMENT FIRST

ORDER ONLINE @ EPLANS.COM

Hamptons

Shingle-style, traditional, and modern—as diverse as these descriptions are, they are each appropriate for this uniquely handsome blending of both the old and the new in The Hamptons. The dramatic setting along the shore of Long Island is unrivaled in its beauty, solitude, serenity, and, paradoxically, its immediate proximity to the city and all that it has to offer. The Hamptons—the best of all worlds, here for you.

© William E. Poole Designs, Inc.

HPK3100086

FIRST FLOOR: 2,746 SQ. FT.
SECOND FLOOR: 992 SQ. FT.
TOTAL: 3,738 SQ. FT.
BONUS SPACE: 453 SQ. FT.
BEDROOMS: 4
BATHROOMS: 3½
WIDTH: 80' - 0"
DEPTH: 58' - 6"
FOUNDATION: CRAWLSPACE

ORDER ONLINE @ EPLANS.COM

Dixie

I have traveled many roads in the tidewater regions, ferreting out the isolated plantation homes that remain. Once, glimpsing a child with his goat cart, I was reminded of my pet goat, Billy, and little brother, A.T. One day, A.T. fed Billy all my Kits. With the candy gone, A.T. ran, but Billy followed right behind him, butting and bawling for more candy all the way home. Reaching the porch and slamming the screen door, A.T. had but one brief moment of escape. Billy burst right through the door and the chase was on again. Memories are stirred in this tidewater region of things past and present, as in this welcoming homeplace—Dixie.

SECOND FLOOR

FIRST FLOOR

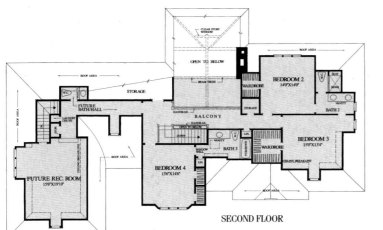

SECOND FLOOR

HPK3100088

First Floor: 2,526 sq. ft.
Second Floor: 1,215 sq. ft.
Total: 3,741 sq. ft.
Bonus Space: 547 sq. ft.
Bedrooms: 4
Bathrooms: 4½ + ½
Width: 88' - 6"
Depth: 53' - 6"
Foundation: Crawlspace

ORDER ONLINE @ EPLANS.COM

Provence

What has come to be known as the "Country French" look is really the style of Provence. A farmhouse with French flourish, never contrived or pretentious, yet comfortable, exquisite, and distinctive, is this regional style. Rural traditions kept alive in small French villages vibrating with "white" sun, pulsating winds, olive groves, and lavender fields embody all that is most French. Afternoons are spent with old and young alike exchanging stories while sipping wine beneath broad trees and at small sidewalk cafes—taking the moment to enjoy life, one day at a time.

FIRST FLOOR

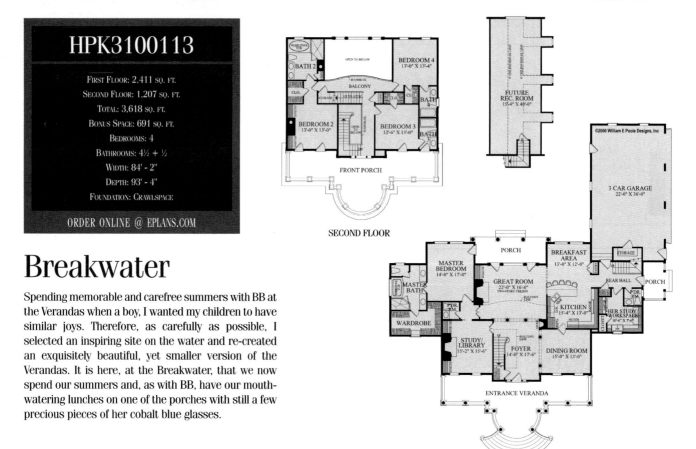

HPK3100113

FIRST FLOOR: 2,411 SQ. FT.

SECOND FLOOR: 1,207 SQ. FT.

TOTAL: 3,618 SQ. FT.

BONUS SPACE: 691 SQ. FT.

BEDROOMS: 4

BATHROOMS: 4½ + ½

WIDTH: 84' - 2"

DEPTH: 93' - 4"

FOUNDATION: Crawlspace

ORDER ONLINE @ EPLANS.COM

Breakwater

Spending memorable and carefree summers with BB at the Verandas when a boy, I wanted my children to have similar joys. Therefore, as carefully as possible, I selected an inspiring site on the water and re-created an exquisitely beautiful, yet smaller version of the Verandas. It is here, at the Breakwater, that we now spend our summers and, as with BB, have our mouth-watering lunches on one of the porches with still a few precious pieces of her cobalt blue glasses.

© William E. Poole Designs, Inc.

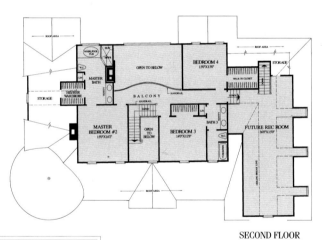

SECOND FLOOR

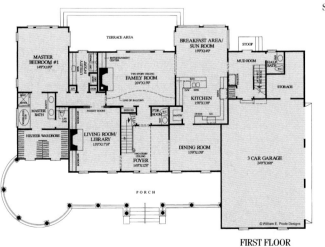

FIRST FLOOR

St. Francisville

If you have never been to St. Francisville, you must go—especially during their annual spring Audubon pilgrimage. This quaint little town is resplendent in color with flowers, flags, costumes from another era, and strolling visitors such as you and me. A welcoming village filled with historic homes such as this, all still there for us to see.

Waverly

The Waverly is a classical Georgian home that, from all appearances, could be either the newest dwelling on the block or the old historic home on whose grounds the surrounding neighborhood was conceived and developed. Proportions and authentic details so handsomely depicted, anchored by twin chimneys—on either side of the impressive center structure, they give one reflective pause upon approaching the Waverly for the first time—as well as all the times in the future when feeling truly welcomed home.

© William E. Poole Designs, Inc.

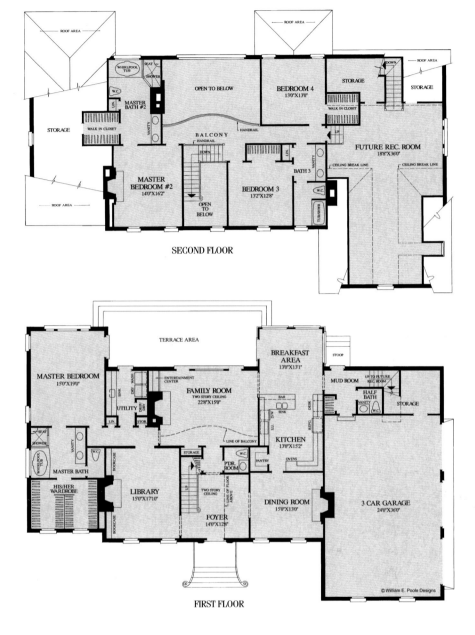

SECOND FLOOR

ROOF AREA

ROOF AREA

ROOF AREA

ROOF AREA

ROOF AREA

STORAGE

WHIRLPOOL TUB

SEAT

SHOWER

W.C.

MASTER BATH #2

LIN.

WALK IN CLOSET

VANITY

OPEN TO BELOW

BEDROOM 4
13'0"X13'0"

STORAGE

DOWN

STORAGE

WALK IN CLOSET

UP

FUTURE REC. ROOM
18'8"X36'0"

BALCONY

HANDRAIL

HANDRAIL

DOWN

MASTER BEDROOM #2
14'0"X16'2"

OPEN TO BELOW

BEDROOM 3
13'2"X12'8"

LIN.

VANITY

BATH 3

W.C.

TUB/SHOWER

CEILING BREAK LINE

CEILING BREAK LINE

FIRST FLOOR

TERRACE AREA

MASTER BEDROOM
15'0"X19'0"

UTILITY

SINK

DRY

WASH

DRIP/DRY

LIN.

STOR.

ENTERTAINMENT CENTER

FAMILY ROOM
TWO STORY CEILING
22'8"X15'0"

BREAKFAST AREA
13'0"X13'1"

STOOP

MUD ROOM

UP TO FUTURE REC. ROOM

HALF BATH

VANITY

W.C.

STORAGE

SEAT

SHOWER

WHIRLPOOL TUB

VANITY

W.C.

MASTER BATH

HIS/HER WARDROBE

BOOKCASE

STORAGE

LINE OF BALCONY

BAR

SINK

D.W.

DESK

REFG.

KITCHEN
13'0"X15'2"

LINE OF FLOOR ABOVE

LIBRARY
15'0"X17'10"

TWO STORY CEILING

UP

FOYER
14'0"X12'8"

PDR. ROOM

W.C.

PANTRY

OVENS

DINING ROOM
15'0"X13'0"

3 CAR GARAGE
24'0"X36'0"

©William E. Poole Designs

© William E. Pool

The Natchez II

The Briars in Natchez, Mississippi, is one of the most sophisticated examples of the planter's cottage architecture of the lower Mississippi Valley, and from the Briars evolved the Natchez. Jefferson Davis married Varina Howell in the parlor of the Briars and one may still visit this beautifully preserved site today. The Natchez II, our most popular home design ever, has struck a universal chord ... thereby inducing many to call it "home."

FUTURE
BEDROOM 5
11'0"X19'0"

ROOF AREA

ROOF AREA

OPEN TO BELOW
CEILING BREAKLINE

BALCONY

WARDROBE

HANDRAIL

VANITY

FUTURE BATH 4

TUB/SHWR.

BEDROOM 2
15'1"X13'0"

LAUNDRY CHUTE

LINEN

STORAGE

DN.

DN.

HANDRAIL

DN.

BEDROOOM 4
16'0"X16'5"

BATH 2

VANITY

BEDROOM 3
15'0"X13'11"

OPEN TO BELOW

CEILING BREAKLINE

TUB/SHWR.

BATH 3

VANITY

WARDROBE

FUTURE REC. ROOM
20'0"X22'8"

CEILING BREAKLINE

ROOF AREA

ROOF AREA

SECOND FLOOR

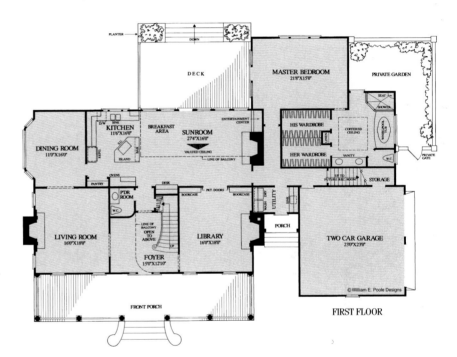

PLANTER

DOWN

DECK

MASTER BEDROOM
21'8"X15'0"

PRIVATE GARDEN

SEAT

SHOWER

D/W

SINK

KITCHEN
11'6"X16'0"

BREAKFAST
AREA

SUNROOM
27'4"X16'0"

ENTERTAINMENT
CENTER

HIS WARDROBE

COFFERED
CEILING

WHIRLPOOL
TUB

PRIVATE
GATE

DINING ROOM
11'0"X16'0"

REF.

BAR

ISLAND

VAULTED CEILING

LINE OF BALCONY

HER WARDROBE

VANITY

W.C.

PANTRY

OVENS

DESK

BOOKCASE

PKT. DOORS

BOOKCASE

FUTURE REC. ROOM

STORAGE

P'DR
ROOM

WASH DRY

UTILITY

SINK

PORCH

W.C.

LINE OF
BALCONY
OPEN
TO
ABOVE

LIBRARY
16'0"X18'0"

LIVING ROOM
16'0"X18'0"

FOYER
15'0"X12'10"

UP

TWO CAR GARAGE
23'0"X23'0"

© William E. Poole Designs

FRONT PORCH

FIRST FLOOR

signs, Inc.

© William E. Poole Designs, Inc.

HPK3100092

First Floor: 2,473 sq. ft.
Second Floor: 1,447 sq. ft.
Total: 3,920 sq. ft.
Bonus Space: 428 sq. ft.
Bedrooms: 4
Bathrooms: 3½
Width: 68' - 8"
Depth: 80' - 0"
Foundation: Crawlspace, Unfinished Walkout Basement

ORDER ONLINE @ EPLANS.COM

Fairfax

As I became old enough to venture away from home, my buddies and I would hike out along Crabtree Creek on Saturday mornings to skinny-dip and pick violets to sell on the Capital Square. After selling just enough flowers for the price of a double-feature matinee, popcorn, and a soda, we would give the rest away. My favorite recipient lived across the square in a classic home that had all the right proportions—balance, and a well-loved glow that made everyone who saw it think, "I always wanted to live in a home just like that!"

SECOND FLOOR

FIRST FLOOR

© William E. Poole Designs, Inc.

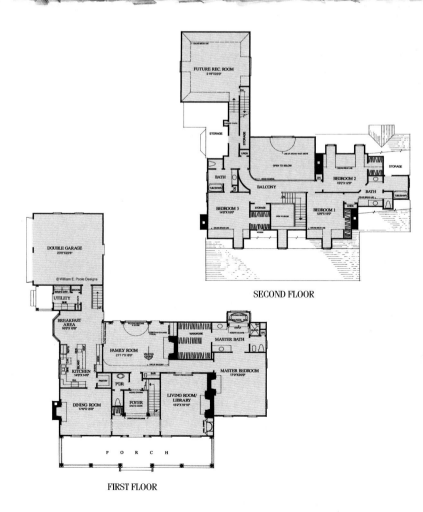

SECOND FLOOR

FIRST FLOOR

The Bel Air

The Garden District of New Orleans is exquisite. The view from the trolley is magical with grand old trees, sweet-smelling vines, clusters and clusters of flowers, and architectural treasures from the bosom of the South. Among these homes sits The Bel Air—down a little side street behind a white picket fence. Ever a reminder of both Louisiana low-county architecture and the gracious manner of living still prevalent there today.

Wyndham

Vintage, yet new—the Wyndham looks seasoned, yet functions for today. It starts out looking good and stays that way. This is a home that was considered "in" in years past, "in" now, and will be "in" years from now. Every neighborhood has a Georgian classic that demands respect and this is just such a house—so stately, with the columned porches to the front of the impressive main body, so circumspect in the correctness of detail, so perfect in every sense of the word.

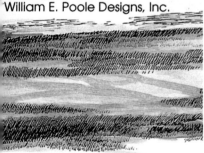

William E. Poole Designs, Inc.

ROOF AREA

STORAGE

TUB/SH-WR

W.C.

BATH 2

VANITY

LINEN

BEDROOM 3
14'0"X12'0"

WALK IN
CLOSET

BEDROOM 4
15'0"X13'8"

CEILING BREAK LINE

VANITY

LINEN

WALK IN
CLOSET

W.C.

BATH 3

FUTURE REC. ROOM
22'0"X18'8"

DOWN

DN.

OPEN TO
BELOW

DOWN

TUB/SHWR

SHLV

LIN

SHLV

STOR.

WALK IN
CLOSET

STORAGE

HANDRAIL

BALCONY

WALK IN
CLOSET

ROOF AREA

BEDROOM 2
15'0"X15'0"

OPEN TO BELOW

BEDROOM 5
15'0"X13'8"

ROOF AREA

SECOND FLOOR

W.C.

VANITY

MASTER
BATH

WHIRLPOOL
TUB

MASTER BEDROOM
14'0"X18'0"

VANITY

SHOWER
SEAT

LIN

SINK

D/W

REFG

HIS/HER
WARDROBE

DRIP/
DRY

BREAKFAST
AREA
11'4"X12'0"

FAMILY ROOM
15'0"X22'0"

STORAGE

WASH DRY

UTILITY
8'4"X8'10"
SINK

SINK

ISLAND
BAR

OVEN

2 CAR GARAGE
22'0"X23'0"

UP TO FUTURE
REC. ROOM

KITCHEN
14'0"X12'0"

PANTRY

OPEN TO
ABOVE

UP

MUD ROOM

DESK

LINE OF BALCONY

PORCH

STOR.

BUTLERS
PANTRY

P'DR
ROOM

FOYER
TWO STORY CEILING
14'0"X15'0"

LIVING ROOM
15'0"X15'0"

©William E. Poole Designs

W.C.

VANITY

DINING ROOM
15'0"X12'0"

PORCH

FIRST FLOOR

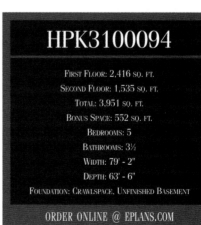

HPK3100094

FIRST FLOOR: 2,416 SQ. FT.
SECOND FLOOR: 1,535 SQ. FT.
TOTAL: 3,951 SQ. FT.
BONUS SPACE: 552 SQ. FT.
BEDROOMS: 5
BATHROOMS: 3½
WIDTH: 79' - 2"
DEPTH: 63' - 6"
FOUNDATION: CRAWLSPACE, UNFINISHED BASEMENT

ORDER ONLINE @ EPLANS.COM

HPK3100095

First Floor: 2,767 sq. ft.

Second Floor: 1,179 sq. ft.

Total: 3,946 sq. ft.

Bonus Space: 591 sq. ft.

Bedrooms: 4

Bathrooms: 3½ + ½

Width: 79' - 11"

Depth: 80' - 6"

Foundation: Crawlspace

ORDER ONLINE @ EPLANS.COM

Evergreen

Memories of Christmases at home with the large tree greeting you upon entering the gracious foyer, garland hanging along the curved staircase, carols being sung around the piano in the library, turkey and pumpkin pie baking in the kitchen—these are what the Evergreen is all about. With its curved and columned front porch, authentic detail, and gracious flow, this "home for all seasons" will welcome family and neighbors throughout the year, and especially for the holidays.

SECOND FLOOR

FIRST FLOOR

© William E. Poole Designs, Inc.

SECOND FLOOR

FIRST FLOOR

HPK3100096

FIRST FLOOR: 2,696 SQ. FT.
SECOND FLOOR: 1,518 SQ. FT.
TOTAL: 4,214 SQ. FT.
BONUS SPACE: 360 SQ. FT.
BEDROOMS: 4
BATHROOMS: 4½ + ½
WIDTH: 72' - 6"
DEPTH: 97' - 10"
FOUNDATION: CRAWLSPACE

ORDER ONLINE @ EPLANS.COM

The Hope Plantation

North Carolina history resounds within the walls of this stately old plantation house. Families, friends, and governing officials all mingled there enjoying the comforts of home, the gaiety of celebrations, and the solemn business of state. Do visit The Hope Plantation and revisit the past so carefully preserved there for generations to come.

Edgewater

On Sundays when we were little, my parents would pile all of us in the car and drive out to the Edgewater, Aunt Clara's house. We had cousins to play with, horses to ride, trees to climb, and fields where we could run with the wind. We loved going to Aunt Clara's—and we loved Aunt Clara.

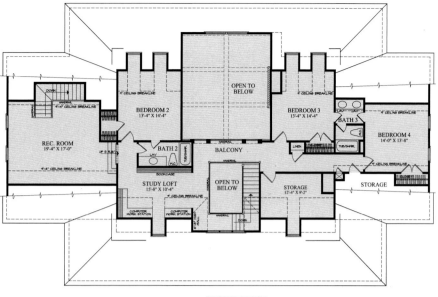

SECOND FLOOR

Second floor rooms:

REC. ROOM
19'-4" X 17'-0"

BEDROOM 2
13'-4" X 14'-4"

OPEN TO BELOW

BEDROOM 3
13'-4" X 14'-4"

BATH 3

BEDROOM 4
14'-0" X 13'-8"

BATH 2

BALCONY

STUDY LOFT
15'-8" X 10'-4"

OPEN TO BELOW

STORAGE
12'-4" X 9'-2"

STORAGE

COMPUTER WORK STATION

COMPUTER WORK STATION

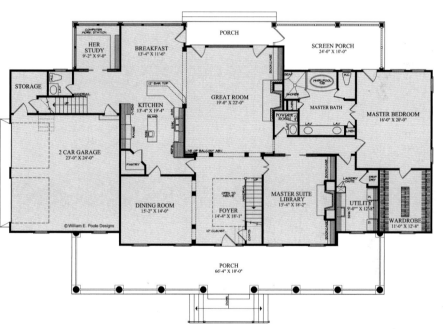

FIRST FLOOR

First floor rooms:

COMPUTER WORK STATION

HER STUDY
9'-2" X 9'-0"

BREAKFAST
13'-4" X 11'-6"

PORCH

SCREEN PORCH
24'-0" X 10'-0"

STORAGE

KITCHEN
13'-4" X 19'-4"

GREAT ROOM
19'-0" X 22'-0"

MASTER BATH

MASTER BEDROOM
16'-0" X 20'-0"

2 CAR GARAGE
23'-0" X 24'-0"

POWDER ROOM

PANTRY

DINING ROOM
15'-2" X 14'-0"

FOYER
14'-4" X 18'-1"

MASTER SUITE LIBRARY
15'-4" X 18'-2"

UTILITY
9'-0" X 12'-8"

WARDROBE
11'-0" X 12'-8"

© William E. Poole Designs

PORCH
66'-4" X 10'-0"

FIRST FLOOR

HPK3100097

FIRST FLOOR: 2,891 SQ. FT.

SECOND FLOOR: 1,336 SQ. FT.

TOTAL: 4,227 SQ. FT.

BONUS SPACE: 380 SQ. FT.

BEDROOMS: 4

BATHROOMS: 3½ + ½

WIDTH: 90' - 8"

DEPTH: 56' - 4"

FOUNDATION: CRAWLSPACE, UNFINISHED BASEMENT

ORDER ONLINE @ EPLANS.COM

Manoir De Bais

The little sidewalk cafe was brimming with activity when excited voices at the next table caught our attention. Noting our interest, they invited us to join them and during the next hour regaled us with myths and legends of an old country home nearby. When during our visit we came upon Manoir de Bais, all the stories we had heard sprang to life. The romance of this Old World French manor remains with us to this very day.

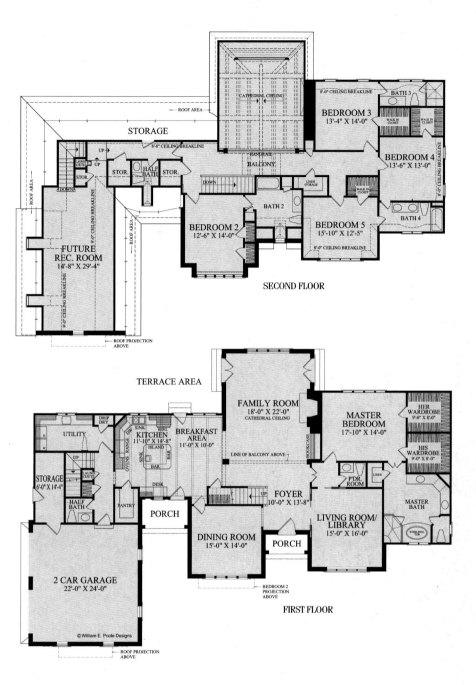

SECOND FLOOR

ROOF AREA

STORAGE

8'-0" CEILING BREAKLINE

BEDROOM 3
13'-4" X 14'-0"

BATH 3

WALK IN CLOSET

WALK IN CLOSET

CATHEDRAL CEILING

8'-0" CEILING BREAKLINE

HANDRAIL

BALCONY

BEDROOM 4
13'-6" X 13'-0"

UP

STOR.

HALF BATH

STOR.

DOWN

LINEN STORAGE

WALK IN CLOSET

DOWNS

BATH 2

BEDROOM 2
12'-6" X 14'-0"

BEDROOM 5
15'-10" X 12'-5"

BATH 4

9'-0" CEILING BREAKLINE

ROOF AREA

FUTURE REC. ROOM
14'-8" X 29'-4"

8'-0" CEILING BREAKLINE

9'-0" CEILING BREAKLINE

ROOF AREA

ROOF PROJECTION ABOVE

FIRST FLOOR

TERRACE AREA

FAMILY ROOM
18'-0" X 22'-0"
CATHEDRAL CEILING

MASTER BEDROOM
17'-10" X 14'-0"

HER WARDROBE
9'-0" X 8'-0"

HIS WARDROBE
9'-0" X 8'-0"

UTILITY

DRIP DRY

SINK

REFG.

KITCHEN
11'-10" X 14'-8"

ISLAND

BREAKFAST AREA
11'-0" X 10'-0"

LINE OF BALCONY ABOVE

BOOKCASE

LINEN

UP

OVENS

RANGE

DW

SINK

BAR

STORAGE
6'-0" X 14'-4"

LAUND. CHUTE

BAR

DESK

PANTRY

HALF BATH

PORCH

FOYER
10'-0" X 13'-8"

UP

P'DR. ROOM

MASTER BATH

2 CAR GARAGE
22'-0" X 24'-0"

DINING ROOM
15'-0" X 14'-0"

PORCH

LIVING ROOM/ LIBRARY
15'-0" X 16'-0"

WHIRLPOOL TUB

BEDROOM 2 PROJECTION ABOVE

© William E. Poole Designs

ROOF PROJECTION ABOVE

HPK3100098

FIRST FLOOR: 2,672 SQ. FT.

SECOND FLOOR: 1,586 SQ. FT.

TOTAL: 4,258 SQ. FT.

BONUS SPACE: 650 SQ. FT.

BEDROOMS: 5

BATHROOMS: 4½ + 2 HALF-BATHS

WIDTH: 89' - 6"

DEPTH: 63' - 0"

FOUNDATION: CRAWLSPACE, UNFINISHED BASEMENT

Shepperd House

Purpose is in the air. Workmen are everywhere. This fine old home is being brought back to life after having been deserted for years. One day, quite by chance, a couple happened by, fell in love with its "bones" and possibilities, and decided to restore the Shepperd House to its former glory. Some stories really do have happy endings. This one surely shall...

© William E. Poole Designs, Inc.

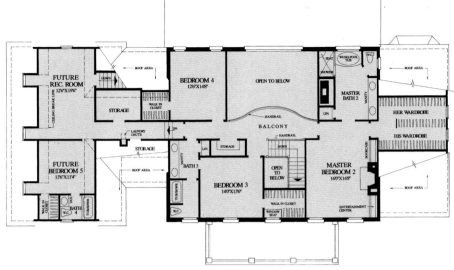

SECOND FLOOR

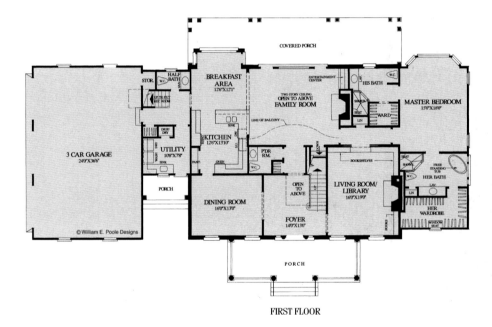

FIRST FLOOR

HPK3100099

First Floor: 2,603 sq. ft.

Second Floor: 1,660 sq. ft.

Total: 4,263 sq. ft.

Bonus Space: 669 sq. ft.

Bedrooms: 4

Bathrooms: 4½ + ½

Width: 98' - 0"

Depth: 56' - 8"

Foundation: Unfinished Basement

ORDER ONLINE @ EPLANS.COM

Savannah

Can you hear it? It's the soft rustle of crinolines beneath the fashionable watered-silk gowns of the county's young Southern belles. As they sashay through the grand entrance of the Savannah, their thoughts turn to the forthcoming festivities. Backyard barbecues held at this stately home are often weekend events that hold a wealth of possibilities. Peeking past the rim of her parasol, she smiles a coy smile—the gentleman from Charleston with the rogue's reputation is making his way toward her. The genteel, Southern way of life is alive at the Savannah.

© William E. Poole Designs, Inc.

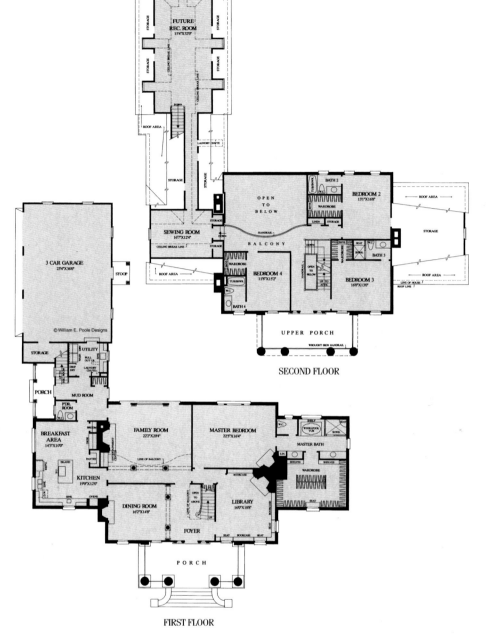

FUTURE REC. ROOM
15'4"X32'0"

3 CAR GARAGE
23'4"X36'0"

SECOND FLOOR

SEWING ROOM
16'7"X12'4"

OPEN TO BELOW

BATH 2

BEDROOM 2
13'1"X16'8"

ROOF AREA

STORAGE

BALCONY

WARDROBE

LINEN

STORAGE

BEDROOM 4
11'8"X15'2"

BEDROOM 3
16'0"X13'0"

BATH 3

BATH 4

UPPER PORCH

WROUGHT IRON HANDRAIL

FIRST FLOOR

STORAGE

UTILITY

LAUNDRY CHUTE

PORCH

MUD ROOM

PDR. ROOM

BREAKFAST AREA
14'3"X10'0"

FAMILY ROOM
22'2"X20'4"

MASTER BEDROOM
22'5"X16'4"

MASTER BATH

WARDROBE

KITCHEN
19'0"X12'0"

ISLAND

PANTRY

DINING ROOM
16'2"X14'8"

FOYER

LIBRARY
16'0"X18'8"

BOOKCASE

PORCH

HPK3100100

First Floor: 2,913 sq. ft.
Second Floor: 1,380 sq. ft.
Total: 4,293 sq. ft.
Bonus Space: 905 sq. ft.
Bedrooms: 4
Bathrooms: 4½
Width: 88' - 4"
Depth: 100' - 8"
Foundation: Crawlspace

ORDER ONLINE @ EPLANS.COM

HPK3100101

First Floor: 3,545 sq. ft.

Second Floor: 2,019 sq. ft.

Total: 5,564 sq. ft.

Bonus Space: 928 sq. ft.

Bedrooms: 4

Bathrooms: 4½ + ½

Width: 124' - 4"

Depth: 79' - 3"

Foundation: Crawlspace, Unfinished Basement

ORDER ONLINE @ EPLANS.COM

Verandas

Papa comes home from the war today. It's been more than a year since we last saw him, and everyone about the house is all aflutter. As Mama busies herself with the maids, preparing for his arrival, I'm outside, pacing back and forth along the porches of Verandas, sipping tea and anxiously awaiting his return. Wait—is that him down by the gate? "Papa! Welcome home!"

SECOND FLOOR

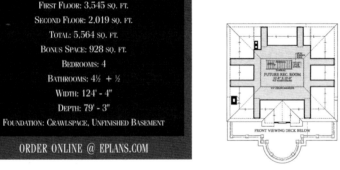

FIRST FLOOR

© William E. Poole Designs, Inc.

SECOND FLOOR

Mount Pleasant

A home on the water. Porches. Cool breezes and golden sunsets. White sails in the distance—gulls drifting overhead. Inner peace. Nothing is more satisfying and fulfilling than home—and home at Mount Pleasant is the stuff from which dreams are made.

FIRST FLOOR

HPK3100103

First Floor: 2,993 sq. ft.

Second Floor: 1,452 sq. ft.

Total: 4,445 sq. ft.

Bonus Space: 611 sq. ft.

Bedrooms: 4

Bathrooms: 5

Width: 113' - 0"

Depth: 65' - 4"

Foundation: Crawlspace

ORDER ONLINE @ EPLANS.COM

SECOND FLOOR

Abbeville

She was an independent woman, a witty and caring soul, and had lived in the Abbeville for so long that she was thought of as "one" with her home. Stories abound ... like the day she was in a hurry, but needed to stop at the bank. Due to an unavailable parking space, she left her car in the middle of the road. A new policeman, not knowing the "dos" and "don'ts" of the small Southern town was stopped in the nick of time from writing her a ticket. The bank president, walking Miss Helen to her car, explained, "She lives in the Abbeville."

FIRST FLOOR

© William E. Poole Designs, Inc.

HPK3100104

FIRST FLOOR: 2,670 SQ. FT.
SECOND FLOOR: 1,795 SQ. FT.
TOTAL: 4,465 SQ. FT.
BONUS SPACE: 744 SQ. FT.
BEDROOMS: 5
BATHROOMS: 4½ + ½
WIDTH: 74' - 8"
DEPTH: 93' - 10"
FOUNDATION: CRAWLSPACE, UNFINISHED BASEMENT

ORDER ONLINE @ EPLANS.COM

The Brewton House

Classical old Southern houses are national treasures and an integral part of our heritage. Such is The Brewton House in Charleston, South Carolina. The history of this house, the town, the family, and the folk from the surrounding area are both fascinating and illuminating—one more connection with our past that remains as a lasting glimpse into our yesteryears.

SECOND FLOOR

FIRST FLOOR

The Ashley

The Ashley, a home of elegant Georgian architecture, is reminiscent of the grand homes in the battery section of Charleston, South Carolina. Horse-drawn carriages pass along the streets, sea gulls circle overhead, and lovers stroll hand-in-hand along the waterfront today, just as they did the day before and the day before that.

PHOTO COURTESY OF WILLIAM E. POOLE DESIGNS, INC. WILMINGTON NC.
THIS HOME, AS SHOWN IN THE PHOTOGRAPH, MAY DIFFER FROM THE ACTUAL BLUEPRINTS. FOR MORE DETAILED INFORMATION, PLEASE CHECK THE FLOOR PLANS CAREFULLY.

FUT. REC ROOM
15'0"X24'0"

ROOF AREA

ROOF AREA

ATTIC STORAGE

ATTIC STORAGE

LAUNDRY CHUTE

DOWN

DOWN

BEDROOM 4
17'0"X13'0"

SINK

W.C.

BATH 3

WARDROBE

W.C.

SINK

BATH 2

LINEN

TUB/SHWR.

SHWR.

ROOF AREA

ATTIC STORAGE

LINEN

WARDROBE

ROOF AREA

BATH 4

TUB/SHWR.

SINK

W.C.

BEDROOM 3
13'6"X14'0"

WOOD RAIL

OPEN
TO
BELOW

DOWN

BEDROOM 2
16'0"X16'0"

ROOF AREA

ROOF AREA

SECOND FLOOR

2 CAR GARAGE
23'0"X24'0"

© William E. Poole Designs

STORAGE

LAUNDRY CHUTE

WASH DRY

UTILITY

FOLD
DN. LR.

MUD ROOM

PORCH

PORCH

PALLADIAN WINDOW

MASTER BEDROOM
18'0"X18'0"

1/2 BATH

W.C.

STO.

ICE MAKER

STORAGE
CLOSET

BOOKCASE

W.C.

LINEN

SHOWER

SU.
REFG.

KITCHEN
16'8"X14'0"

ISLAND

SINK

ENTERTAINMENT
CENTER

FAMILY ROOM
21'0"X17'0"

SINK

PDR. ROOM

STUDY
13'6"X11'0"

MASTER BATH

WHIRLPOOL
TUB

BREAKFAST BAR

PANTRY

BREAKFAST AREA
12'8"X11'0"

CHINA

DINING ROOM
16'0"X14'0"

SILVER

FOYER

UP

LIBRARY
16'0"X16'0"

BOOKCASE

HER WARDROBE

HIS WARDROBE

PORCH

FIRST FLOOR

HPK3100105

FIRST FLOOR: 2,968 SQ. FT.

SECOND FLOOR: 1,521 SQ. FT.

TOTAL: 4,489 SQ. FT.

BONUS SPACE: 522 SQ. FT.

BEDROOMS: 4

BATHROOMS: 4½ + ½

WIDTH: 82' - 6"

DEPTH: 81' - 8"

FOUNDATION: CRAWLSPACE

ORDER ONLINE @ EPLANS.COM

Winchester

The family was gathering at the Winchester. As soon as the car doors opened, the children ran gleefully to see their grandparents—leaving their mother and father to struggle with the luggage, toys, and presents. It was a special homecoming—different from all the ones before—for it marked Mama and Papa's 50th anniversary, and everyone was coming home to celebrate.

© William E. Poole Designs

UNFINISHED ATTIC STORAGE

ROOF AREA · ROOF AREA

DOWN

ROOF AREA · ROOF AREA

ROOF AREA · ROOF AREA

STORAGE

BEDROOM 3
17'-0" X 13'-0"

BATH 3

WALK-IN CLOSET · WALK-IN CLOSET

BEDROOM 4
17'-0" X 13'-0"

STORAGE

COPPER ROOF

WALK-IN CLOSET · LINEN

DOWN · HANDRAIL

BATH 4

— ROOF AREA —

BEDROOM 2
16'-0" X 15'-0"

OPEN TO BELOW

BEDROOM 5
14'-6" X 13'-0"

— ROOF AREA —

BATH 2

COPPER ROOF

SECOND FLOOR

2 CAR GARAGE
23'-0" X 35'-4"

STORAGE

STORAGE · UP

BREAKFAST AREA
16'-0" X 12'-0"

REF'G · VEG. SINK

KITCHEN
16'-0" X 14'-8"

SINK · DW · ISLAND · BAR · DESK

OVEN · S.U.

FAMILY ROOM
23'-8" X 17'-0"

STORAGE

BOOKCASE

PDR. ROOM

LIBRARY
13'-0" X 13'-0"

MASTER BEDROOM
18'-0" X 16'-8"

LINEN · PORCH

MASTER BATH

WASH TRAY · FOLD IN IRON.BD.

UTILITY

SINK · PANTRY

DINING ROOM
16'-0" X 15'-0"

STORAGE

UP · BOOKCASE

STOR. BOOKCASE

LIVING ROOM
15'-0" X 15'-0"

WARDROBE

LINE OF WALL ABOVE

FOYER
12'-8" X 11'-2"

PORCH
13'-0" X 6'-6"

FIRST FLOOR

Designs, Inc.

HPK3100106

First Floor: 3,027 sq. ft.

Second Floor: 1,509 sq. ft.

Total: 4,536 sq. ft.

Bedrooms: 5

Bathrooms: 4½

Width: 85' - 0"

Depth: 82' - 6"

Foundation: Crawlspace, Unfinished Basement

ORDER ONLINE @ EPLANS.COM

© William E. Poole Desig

Marshlands

While taking a ride on the "Natchez," a paddle-wheel boat on the lower Mississippi, the shoreline on either side of the river becomes vivid with both past and present. The Marshlands, in its understated, solid beauty, sits agelessly and serenely in a field of colorful wildflowers. Beckoning up memories of how as children we would run with the butterflies, wade in the river, and picnic on the rocks. Oh, what this raised cottage on the Old Mississippi reawakened in me...

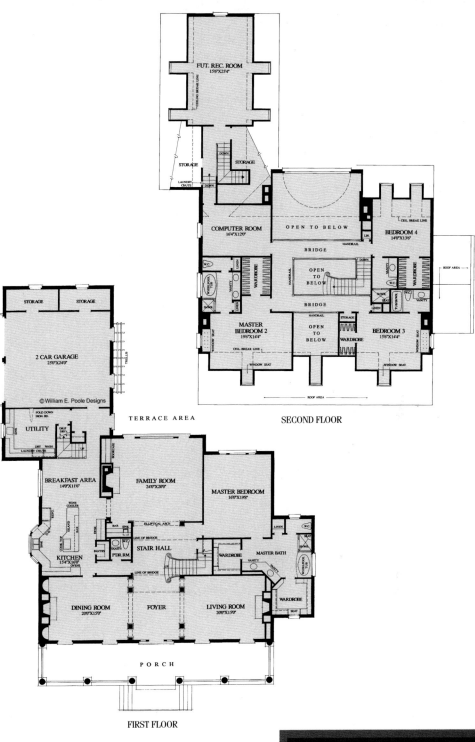

FUT. REC. ROOM
15'6"X25'4"

STORAGE   STORAGE

LAUNDRY
CHUTE   DOWN

COMPUTER ROOM
16'4"X12'0"

OPEN TO BELOW

BEDROOM 4
14'0"X13'6"

ROOF AREA

BRIDGE

HANDRAIL

W.C.

WARDROBE   OPEN TO BELOW   DOWN   WARDROBE

BRIDGE

HANDRAIL   STORAGE

MASTER
BEDROOM 2
19'6"X14'4"   OPEN TO BELOW   WARDROBE   BEDROOM 3
15'6"X14'4"

WINDOW SEAT   CEIL. BREAK LINE

WINDOW SEAT   WINDOW SEAT

ROOF AREA

SECOND FLOOR

STORAGE   STORAGE

2 CAR GARAGE
25'0"X24'0"

©William E. Poole Designs

TERRACE AREA

FOLD DOWN
IRON. BD.

UTILITY

DRY.   WASH.

LAUNDRY CHUTE

BREAKFAST AREA
14'0"X11'6"

WINE
COOLER

KITCHEN
15'4"X16'0"

ISLAND   BAR

COOK TOP   OVENS   BAR

DESK

BOOKCASE

FAMILY ROOM
24'0"X20'0"

ELLIPTICAL ARCH

LINE OF BRIDGE

STAIR HALL

LINE OF BRIDGE

MASTER BEDROOM
16'0"X19'8"

LINEN   W.C.

WARDROBE   MASTER BATH

VANITY   DOWN

DINING ROOM
20'0"X15'0"   FOYER   LIVING ROOM
20'0"X15'0"   WARDROBE

SEAT

PORCH

FIRST FLOOR

Sycamores

"Of course I know you two. You're the girls who live at Sycamores." Nodding our heads in the affirmative, we smiled and waited patiently astride our mounts while she went inside to prepare us a snack. Unbeknownst to us, she called our aunt. In short order there was a squeal of tires, a churning of dust, and a roar of a car charging up the drive. Earlier that morning we had impulsively decided to travel a bit, so we bridled the mules and rode bareback down a country road until we became hungry. Our aunt saw to it that our traveling days were over for the rest of that summer and, if you've ever ridden a mule, then you know our sitting days were over for a good while too.

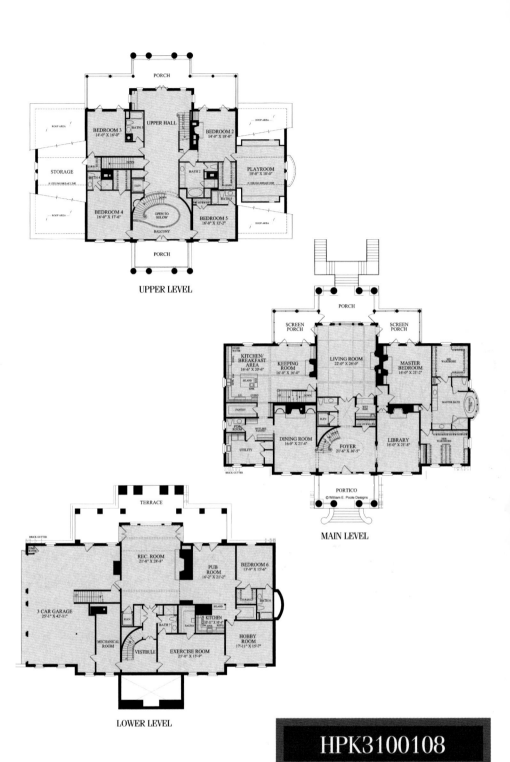

UPPER LEVEL

PORCH

BEDROOM 3
14'-0" X 16'-0"

UPPER HALL

BATH 3

BEDROOM 2
14'-0" X 18'-0"

ROOF AREA

STORAGE

BATH 4

PLAYROOM
18'-0" X 18'-0"

ROOF AREA

BEDROOM 4
16'-0" X 17'-6"

OPEN TO BELOW

ELEV.

BEDROOM 5
16'-0" X 12'-2"

ROOF AREA

BALCONY

PORCH

MAIN LEVEL

PORCH

SCREEN PORCH

SCREEN PORCH

KITCHEN/
BREAKFAST
AREA
16'-6" X 20'-6"

KEEPING
ROOM
16'-0" X 16'-0"

LIVING ROOM
22'-0" X 26'-0"

MASTER
BEDROOM
16'-0" X 21'-2"

PANTRY

DINING ROOM
16'-0" X 21'-4"

FOYER
21'-6" X 16'-5"

LIBRARY
16'-0" X 21'-8"

MASTER BATH

UTILITY

PORTICO

© William E. Poole Designs

LOWER LEVEL

TERRACE

REC. ROOM
21'-8" X 28'-8"

PUB
ROOM
16'-2" X 21'-2"

BEDROOM 6
13'-9" X 15'-6"

3 CAR GARAGE
25'-1" X 42'-11"

KITCHEN

BATH 6

MECHANICAL
ROOM

BATH 7

SAUNA

HOBBY
ROOM
17'-11" X 15'-7"

VESTIBULE

EXERCISE ROOM
25'-0" X 13'-9"

HPK3100108

MAIN LEVEL: 4,556 SQ. FT.

UPPER LEVEL: 3,261 SQ. FT.

LOWER LEVEL: 2,918 SQ. FT.

TOTAL: 10,735 SQ. FT.

BEDROOMS: 6

BATHROOMS: 7½ + ½

WIDTH: 97' - 2"

DEPTH: 81' - 2"

FOUNDATION: Finished Walkout Basement

ORDER ONLINE @ EPLANS.COM

Richmond Hill

High atop a hill overlooking the James River sits a grand and glorious plantation house, the Richmond Hill. The spectacular view of stars, moon, and twinkling lights from the town below entrances visitors from far and near as they gather each evening to recount the adventures of their day and delight in the promise of the night.

SECOND FLOOR

FIRST FLOOR

HPK3100109

First Floor: 3,635 sq. ft.

Second Floor: 1,357 sq. ft.

Total: 4,992 sq. ft.

Bonus Space: 759 sq. ft.

Bedrooms: 4

Bathrooms: 4½ + ½

Width: 121' - 6"

Depth: 60' - 4"

Foundation: Crawlspace, Unfinished Basement

ORDER ONLINE @ EPLANS.COM

Longview

Home extraordinaire ... with regency and Colonial Revival architectural characteristics, the Longview is a house of elegance and comfort, a home that combines the best of architecture and design—a refined home that exudes both excitement and warmth. The Longview was designed and built as a Classic American Homes Lifestyle Showcase. Inside and out, the Longview is romantic and extraordinary and, because of the classical designs of both the home and the furnishings, it is timeless—a trait that is distinctly "Poole."

SECOND FLOOR

FIRST FLOOR

HPK3100110

First Floor: 3,463 sq. ft.

Second Floor: 1,924 sq. ft.

Total: 5,387 sq. ft.

Bedrooms: 4

Bathrooms: 5½

Width: 88' - 6"

Depth: 98' - 0"

Foundation: Crawlspace, Finished Basement,
Unfinished Basement

ORDER ONLINE @ EPLANS.COM

Turn Your
Dream Home
Into A Reality

Our home styles collection offers distinctive design coupled with plans to match every wallet. If you are looking to build your new home, look to Hanley Wood first.

Pick up a Copy Today!

Finding the right new home to fit

- Your style
- Your budget
- Your life

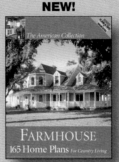
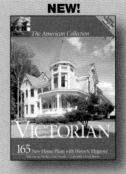
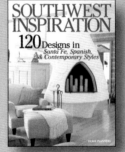

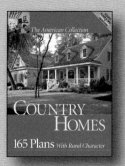

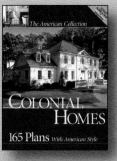

AMERICAN COLLECTION:
Craftsman

Celebrate the fine details and modest proportions of the Craftsman style with this beautiful collection of 165 homes.

$10.95 U.S.
ISBN-10: 1-931131-54-6
ISBN-13: 978-1-931131-54-4
192 full-color pages

AMERICAN COLLECTION:
Country

The American Collection: Country is a must-have if you're looking to build a country home or if you want to bring the relaxed country spirit into your current home.

$10.95 U.S.
ISBN-10: 1-931131-35-X
192 full-color pages

AMERICAN COLLECTION:
Colonial

This beautiful collection features distinctly American home styles—find everything from Colonial, Cape Cod, Georgian, Farmhouse or Saltbox.

$10.95 U.S.
ISBN-10: 1-931131-40-6
192 full-color pages

NEW!

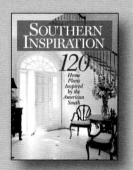

William E. Poole's American Home

This new collection of 110 house plans will encapsulate the simplicity, beauty, and traditional designs that have made plans from William E. Poole among the most treasured homes in the country.

$18.95 U.S.
ISBN-10: 1-931131-64-3
ISBN-13: 978-1-931131-64-3
192 pages

Southern Inspiration

The comfortable and luxurious home styles of the American South are highlighted in this new title. Georgian, Federal, Floridian, and other styles feature prominently in this exclusively Southern collection.

$14.95 U.S.
ISBN-10: 1-931131-41-4
192 full-color pages

Provençal Inspiration

This title features home plans, landscapes and interior plans that evoke the French Country spirit.

$14.95 U.S.
ISBN-10: 1-881955-89-3
192 full-color pages

Hanley Wood provides the largest selection of plans from the nation's top designers and architects. Our special home styles collection offers designs to suit any taste.

With more than 50 years of experience in the industry and millions of blueprints sold, Hanley Wood is a trusted source of high-quality, high-value pre-drawn home plans.

Using pre-drawn home plans is a **reliable, cost-effective way** to build your dream home, and our vast selection of plans is second-to-none. The nation's finest designers craft these plans that builders know they can trust. Meanwhile, our friendly, knowledgeable customer service representatives can help you every step of the way.

WHAT YOU'LL GET WITH YOUR ORDER

The contents of each designer's blueprint package is unique, but all contain detailed, high-quality working drawings. You can expect to find the following standard elements in most sets of plans:

I. FRONT PERSPECTIVE

This artist's sketch of the exterior of the house gives you an idea of how the house will look when built and landscaped.

2. FOUNDATION AND BASEMENT PLANS

This sheet shows the foundation layout including concrete walls, footings, pads, posts, beams, bearing walls, and foundation notes. If the home features a basement, the first-floor framing details may also be included on this plan. If your plan features slab construction rather than a basement, the plan shows footings and details for a monolithic slab. This page, or another in the set, may include a sample plot plan for locating your house on a building site. Additional sheets focus on foundation cross-sections and other details.

3. DETAILED FLOOR PLANS

These plans show the layout of each floor of the house. Rooms and interior spaces are carefully dimensioned, doors and windows located, and keys are given for cross-section details provided elsewhere in the plans.

4. HOUSE AND DETAIL CROSS-SECTIONS

Large-scale views show sections or cutaways of the foundation, interior walls, exterior walls, floors, stairways, and roof details. Additional cross-sections may show important changes in floor, ceiling, or roof heights, or the relationship of one level to another. These sections show exactly how the various parts of the house fit together and are extremely valuable during construction. Additional sheets may include enlarged wall, floor, and roof construction details.

5. FLOOR STRUCTURAL SUPPORTS

The floor framing plans provide detail for these crucial elements of your home. Each includes floor joist, ceiling joist, spacing, direction, span, and specifications. Beam and window headers, along with necessary details for framing connections, stairways, or dormers are also included.

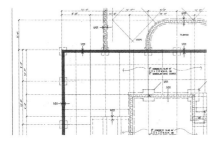

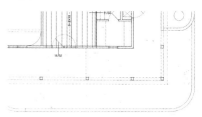

6. ELECTRICAL PLAN

The electrical plan offers suggested locations with notes for all lighting, outlets, switches, and circuits. A layout is provided for each level, as well as basements, garages, or other structures. This plan does not contain diagrams detailing how all wiring should be run, or how circuits should be engineered. These details should be designed by your electrician.

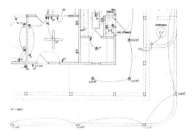

7. EXTERIOR ELEVATIONS

In addition to the front exterior, your blueprint set will include drawings of the rear and sides of your house as well. These drawings give notes on exterior materials and finishes. Particular attention is given to cornice detail, brick and stone accents, or other finish items that make your home unique.

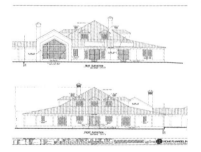

ROOF FRAMING PLANS — PLEASE READ

Some plans contain roof framing plans; however because of the wide variation in local requirements, many plans do not. If you buy a plan without a roof framing plan, you will need an engineer familiar with local building codes to create a plan to build your roof. Even if your plan does contain a roof framing plan, we recommend that a local engineer review the plan to verify that it will meet local codes.

BEFORE YOU CALL

You are making a terrific decision to use a pre-drawn house plan—it is one you can make with confidence, knowing that your blueprints are crafted by national-award-winning certified residential designers and architects, and trusted by builders.

Once you've selected the plan you want—or even if you have questions along the way—our experienced customer service representatives are available 24 hours a day, seven days a week to help you navigate the home-building process. To help them provide you with even better service, please consider the following questions before you call:

■ Have you chosen or purchased your lot?
If so, please review the building setback requirements of your local building authority before you call. You don't need to have a lot before ordering plans, but if you own land already, please have the width and depth dimensions handy when you call.

■ Have you chosen a builder?
Involving your builder in the plan selection and evaluation process may be beneficial. Luckily, builders know they can have confidence with pre-drawn plans because they've been designed for livability, functionality, and typically are builder-proven at successful home sites across the country.

■ Do you need a construction loan?
Construction loans are unique because they involve determining the value of something that is not yet constructed. Several lenders offer convenient contstruction-to-permanent loans. It is important to choose a good lending partner—one who will help guide you through the application and appraisal process. Most will even help you evaluate your contractor to ensure reliability and credit worthiness. Our partnership with IndyMac Bank, a nationwide leader in construction loans, can help you save on your loan, if needed (see the next page for details).

■ How many sets of plans do you need?
Building a home can typically require a number of sets of blueprints—one for yourself, two or three for the builder and subcontractors, two for the local building department, and one or more for your lender. For this reason, we offer 5- and 8-set plan packages, but your best value is the Reproducible Plan Package. Reproducible plans are accompanied by a license to make modifications and typically up to 12 duplicates of the plan so you have enough copies of the plan for everyone involved in the financing and construction of your home.

■ Do you want to make any changes to the plan?
We understand that it is difficult to find blueprints for a home that will meet all of your needs. That is why Hanley Wood is glad to offer plan Customization Services. We will work with you to design the modifications you'd like to see and to adjust your blueprint plans accordingly—anything from changing the foundation; adding square footage, redesigning baths, kitchens, or bedrooms; or most other modifications. This simple, cost-effective service saves you from hiring an outside architect to make alterations. Modifications may only be made to Reproducible Plan Packages that include the license to modify.

■ Do you have to make any changes to meet local building codes?
While all of our plans are drawn to meet national building codes at the time they were created, many areas required that plans be stamped by a local engineer to certify that they meet local building codes. Building codes are updated frequently and can vary by state, county, city, or municipality. Contact your local building inspection department, office of planning and zoning, or department of permits to determine how your local codes will affect your construction project. The best way to assure that you can make changes to your plan, if necessary, is to purchase a Reproducible Plan Package.

■ Has everyone—from family members to contractors—been involved in selecting the plan?
Building a new home is an exciting process, and using pre-drawn plans is a great way to realize your dreams. Make sure that everyone involved has had an opportunity to review the plan you've selected. While Hanley Wood is the only plans provider with an exchange policy, it's best to be sure all parties agree on your selection before you buy.

CALL TOLL-FREE 1-800-521-6797

Source Key
HPK31

CUSTOMIZE YOUR PLAN – HANLEY WOOD CUSTOMIZATION SERVICES

Creating custom home plans has never been easier and more directly accessible. Using state-of-the-art technology and top-performing architectural expertise, Hanley Wood delivers on a long-standing customer commitment to provide world-class home-plans and customization services. Our valued customers—professional home builders and individual home owners—appreciate the convenience and accessibility of this interactive, consultative service.

With the Hanley Wood Customization Service you can:

■ Save valuable time by avoiding drawn-out and frequently repetitive face-to-face design meetings

■ Communicate design and home-plan changes faster and more efficiently
■ Speed-up project turn-around time
■ Build on a budget without sacrificing quality
■ Transform master home plans to suit your design needs and unique personal style

All of our design options and prices are impressively affordable. A detailed quote is available for a $50 consultation fee. Plan modification is an interactive service. Our skilled team of designers will guide you through the customization process from start to finish making recommendations, offering ideas, and determining the feasibility of your changes. This level of service is offered to ensure the final modified plan meets your expectations. If you use our service the $50 fee will be applied to the cost of the modifications.

You may purchase the customization consultation before or after purchasing a plan. In either case, it is necessary to purchase the Reproducible Plan Package and complete the accompanying license to modify the plan before we can begin customization.

Customization Consultation **$50**

TOOLS TO WORK WITH YOUR BUILDER

Two Reverse Options For Your Convenience – Mirror and Right-Reading Reverse (as available)

Mirror reverse plans simply flip the design 180 degrees—keep in mind, the text will also be flipped. For a minimal fee you can have one or all of your plans shipped mirror reverse, although we recommend having at least one regular set handy. Right-reading reverse plans show the design flipped 180 degrees but the text reads normally. When you choose this option, we ship each set of purchased blueprints in this format.

Mirror Reverse Fee (indicate the number of sets when ordering) $55
Right Reading Reverse Fee (all sets are reversed) $175

A Shopping List Exclusively for Your Home – Materials List

A customized Materials List helps you plan and estimate the cost of your new home, outlining the quantity, type, and size of materials needed to build your house (with the exception of mechanical system items). Included are framing lumber, windows and doors, kitchen and bath cabinetry, rough and finished hardware, and much more.

Materials List . . . .**$85 each**
Additional Materials Lists (at original time of purchase only)$20 each

Plan Your Home-Building Process – Specification Outline

Work with your builder on this step-by-step chronicle of 166 stages or items crucial to the building process. It provides a comprehensive review of the construction process and helps you choose materials.
Specification Outline . . . .**$10 each**

Get Accurate Cost Estimates for Your Home – Quote One® Cost Reports

The Summary Cost Report, the first element in the Quote One® package, breaks down the cost of your home into various categories based on building materials, labor, and installation, and includes three grades of construction: Budget, Standard, and Custom. Make even more informed decisions about your project with the second element of our package, the Material Cost Report. The material and installation cost is shown for each of more than 1,000 line items provided in the standard-grade Materials List, which is included with this tool. Additional space is included for estimates from contractors and subcontractors, such as for mechanical materials, which are not included in our packages.

Quote One® Summary Cost Report **$35**
Quote One® Detailed Material Cost Report **$140***
***Detailed material cost report includes the Materials List**

Learn the Basics of Building – Electrical, Pluming, Mechanical, Construction Detail Sheets

If you want to know more about building techniques—and deal more confidently with your subcontractors—we offer four useful detail sheets. These sheets provide non-plan-specific general information, but are excellent tools that will add to your understanding of Plumbing Details, Electrical Details, Construction Details, and Mechanical Details.

Electrical Detail Sheet **$14.95**
Plumbing Detail Sheet **$14.95**
Mechanical Detail Sheet **$14.95**
Construction Detail Sheet **$14.95**

SUPER VALUE SETS:
Buy any 2: $26.95; Buy any 3: $34.95; Buy All 4: $39.95

Best Value

GETTY IMAGES (2)

MAKE YOUR HOME TECH-READY – HOME AUTOMATION UPGRADE

Building a new home provides a unique opportunity to wire it with a plan for future needs. A Home Automation-Ready (HA-Ready) home contains the wiring substructure of tomorrow's connected home. It means that every room—from the front porch to the backyard, and from the attic to the basement—is wired for security, lighting, telecommunications, climate control, home computer networking, whole-house audio, home theater, shade control, video surveillance, entry access control, and yes, video gaming electronic solutions.

Along with the conveniences HA-Ready homes provide, they also have a higher resale value. The Consumer Electronics Association (CEA), in conjunction with the Custom Electronic Design and Installation Association (CEDIA), have developed a TechHome™ Rating system that quantifies the value of HA-Ready homes. The rating system is gaining widespread recognition in the real estate industry.

Developed by CEDIA-certified installers, our Home Automation Upgrade package includes everything you need to work with an installer during the construction of your home. It provides a short explanation of the various subsystems, a wiring floor plan for each level of your home, a detailed materials list with estimated costs, and a list of CEDIA-certified installers in your local area.
Home Automation Upgrade $250

GET YOUR HOME PLANS PAID FOR!

IndyMac Bank, in partnership with Hanley Wood, will reimburse you up to $1,000 toward the cost of your home plans simply by financing the construction of your new home with IndyMac Bank Home Construction Lending.

IndyMac's construction and permanent loan is a one-time close loan, meaning that one application—and one set of closing fees—provides all the financing you need.

Apply today at www.indymacbank.com, call toll free at 1-800-847-6138, or ask a Hanley Wood customer service representative for details.

DESIGN YOUR HOME – INTERIOR AND EXTERIOR FINISHING TOUCHES

Be Your Own Interior Designer! – Home Furniture Planner

Effectively plan the space in your home using our Hands-On Home Furniture Planner. It's fun and easy—no more moving heavy pieces of furniture to see how the room will go together. The kit includes reusable peel-and-stick furniture templates that fit on a 12"x18" laminated layout board—enough space to lay out every room in your house.
Home Furniture Planning Kit **$15.95**

Enjoy the Outdoors! – Deck Plans

Many of our homes have a corresponding deck plan, sold separately, which includes a Deck Plan Frontal Sheet, Deck Framing and Floor Plans, Deck Elevations, and a Deck Materials List. A Standard Deck Details Package, also available, provides all the how-to information necessary for building any deck. Get both the Deck Plan and the Standard Deck Details Package for one low price in our Complete Deck Building Package. See the price tier chart below and call for deck plan availability.
Deck Details (only) **$14.95**
Deck Building Package . . . . **Plan price + $14.95**

Create a Professionally Designed Landscape – Landscape Plans

Many of our homes have a front-yard Landscape Plan that is complementary in design to the house plan. These comprehensive Landscape Blueprint Packages include a Frontal Sheet, Plan View, Regionalized Plant & Materials List, a sheet on Planting and Maintaining Your Landscape, Zone Maps, and a Plant Size and Description Guide. Each set of blueprints is a full 18" x 24" with clear, complete instructions in easy-to-read type. Our Landscape Plans are available with a Plant & Materials List adapted by horticultural experts to eight regions of the country. Please specify your region when ordering your plan—see region map below. Call for more information about landscape plan availability and applicable regions.

LANDSCAPE & DECK PRICE SCHEDULE

PRICE TIERS	1-SET STUDY PACKAGE	5-SET BUILDING PACKAGE	8-SET BUILDING PACKAGE	1-SET REPRODUCIBLE*
P1	$25	$55	$95	$145
P2	$45	$75	$115	$165
P3	$75	$105	$145	$195
P4	$105	$135	$175	$225
P5	$175	$205	$305	$405
P6	$215	$245	$345	$445

PRICES SUBJECT TO CHANGE * REQUIRES A FAX NUMBER

TERMS & CONDITIONS

OUR 90-DAY EXCHANGE POLICY

BUY WITH CONFIDENCE!

Hanley Wood is committed to ensuring your satisfaction with your blueprint order, which is why we offer a 90-day exchange policy. With the exception of Reproducible Plan Package orders, we will exchange your entire first order for an equal or greater number of blueprints from our plan collection within 90 days of the original order. The entire content of your original order must be returned before an exchange will be processed. Please call our customer service department at 1-888-690-1116 for your return authorization number and shipping instructions. If the returned blueprints look used, redlined, or copied, we will not honor your exchange. Fees for exchanging your blueprints are as follows: 20% of the amount of the original order, plus the difference in cost if exchanging for a design in a higher price bracket or less the difference in cost if exchanging for a design in a lower price bracket. (Because they can be copied, Reproducible blueprints are not exchangeable or refundable.) Please call for current postage and handling prices. Shipping and handling charges are not refundable.

ARCHITECTURAL AND ENGINEERING SEALS

Some cities and states now require that a licensed architect or engineer review and "seal" a blueprint, or officially approve it, prior to construction. Prior to application for a building permit or the start of actual construction, we strongly advise that you consult your local building official who can tell you if such a review is required.

LOCAL BUILDING CODES AND ZONING REQUIREMENTS

Each plan was designed to meet or exceed the requirements of a nationally recognized model building code in effect at the time and place the plan was drawn. Typically plans designed after the year 2000 conform to the International Residential Building Code (IRC 2000 or 2003). The IRC is comprised of portions of the three major codes below. Plans drawn before 2000 conform to one of the three recognized building codes in effect at the time: Building Officials and Code Administrators (BOCA) International, Inc.;

**CALL TOLL-FREE
1-800-521-6797
OR VISIT
EPLANS.COM**

the Southern Building Code Congress International, (SBCCI) Inc.; the International Conference of Building Officials (ICBO); or the Council of American Building Officials (CABO).

Because of the great differences in geography and climate throughout the United States and Canada, each state, county, and municipality has its own building codes, zone requirements, ordinances, and building regulations. Your plan may need to be modified to comply with local requirements. In addition, you may need to obtain permits or inspections from local governments before and in the course of construction. We authorize the use of the blueprints on the express condition that you consult a local licensed architect or engineer of your choice prior to beginning construction and strictly comply with all local building codes, zoning requirements, and other applicable laws, regulations, ordinances, and requirements. Notice: Plans for homes to be built in Nevada must be redrawn by a Nevada-registered professional. Consult your local building official for more information on this subject.

TERMS AND CONDITIONS

These designs are protected under the terms of United States Copyright Law and may not be copied or reproduced in any way, by

any means, unless you have purchased a Reproducible Plan Package and signed the accompanying license to modify and copy the plan, which clearly indicates your right to modify, copy, or reproduce. We authorize the use of your chosen design as an aid in the construction of ONE (1) single- or multifamily home only. You may not use this design to build a second dwelling or multiple dwellings without purchasing another blueprint or blueprints or paying additional design fees. Multi-use fees vary by designer—please call one of experienced sales representatives for a quote.

DISCLAIMER

The designers we work with have put substantial care and effort into the creation of their blueprints. However, because we cannot provide on-site consultation, supervision, and control over actual construction, and because of the great variance in local building requirements, building practices, and soil, seismic, weather, and other conditions, WE MAKE NO WARRANTY OF ANY KIND, EXPRESS OR IMPLIED, WITH RESPECT TO THE CONTENT OR USE OF THE BLUEPRINTS, INCLUDING BUT NOT LIMITED TO ANY WARRANTY OF MERCHANTABILITY OR OF FITNESS FOR A PARTICULAR PURPOSE. ITEMS, PRICES, TERMS, AND CONDITIONS ARE SUBJECT TO CHANGE WITHOUT NOTICE.

IMPORTANT COPYRIGHT NOTICE

From the Council of Publishing Home Designers

Blueprints for residential construction (or working drawings, as they are often called in the industry) are copyrighted intellectual property, protected under the terms of the United States Copyright Law and, therefore, cannot be copied legally for use in building. The following are some guidelines to help you get what you need to build your home, without violating copyright law:

1. HOME PLANS ARE COPYRIGHTED

Just like books, movies, and songs, home plans receive protection under the federal copyright laws. The copyright laws prevent anyone, other than the copyright owner, from reproducing, modifying, or reusing the plans or design without permission of the copyright owner.

2. DO NOT COPY DESIGNS OR FLOOR PLANS FROM ANY PUBLICATION, ELECTRONIC MEDIA, OR EXISTING HOME

It is illegal to copy, change, or redraw home designs found in a plan book, CDROM or on the Internet. The right to modify plans is one of the exclusive rights of copyright. It is also illegal to copy or redraw a constructed home that is protected by copyright, even if you have never seen the plans for the home. If you find a plan or home that you like, you must purchase a set of plans from an authorized source. The plans may not be lent, given away, or sold by the purchaser.

3. DO NOT USE PLANS TO BUILD MORE THAN ONE HOUSE

The original purchaser of house plans is typically licensed to build a single home from the plans. Building more than one home from the plans without permission is an infringement of the home designer's copyright. The purchase of a multiple-set package of plans is for the construction of a single home only. The purchase of additional sets of plans does not grant the right to construct more than one home.

4. HOUSE PLANS IN THE FORM OF BLUEPRINTS OR BLACKLINES CANNOT BE COPIED OR REPRODUCED

Plans, blueprints, or blacklines, unless they are reproducibles, cannot be copied or reproduced without prior written consent of the copyright owner. Copy shops and blueprinters are prohibited from making copies of these plans without the copyright release letter you receive with reproducible plans.

5. HOUSE PLANS IN THE FORM OF BLUEPRINTS OR BLACKLINES CANNOT BE REDRAWN

Plans cannot be modified or redrawn without first obtaining the copyright owner's permission. With your purchase of plans, you are licensed to make nonstructural changes by "red-lining" the purchased plans. If you need to make structural changes or need to redraw the plans for any reason, you must purchase a reproducible set of plans (see topic 6) which includes a license to modify the plans. Blueprints do not come with a license to make structural changes or to redraw the plans. You may not reuse or sell the modified design.

6. REPRODUCIBILE HOME PLANS

Reproducible plans (for example sepias, mylars, CAD files, electronic files, and vellums) come with a license to make modifications to the plans. Once modified, the plans can be taken to a local copy shop or blueprinter to make up to 10 or 12 copies of the plans to use in the construction of a single home. Only one home can be constructed from any single purchased set of reproducible plans either in original form or as modified. The license to modify and copy must be completed and returned before the plan will be shipped.

7. MODIFIED DESIGNS CANNOT BE REUSED

Even if you are licensed to make modifications to a copyrighted design, the modified design is not free from the original designer's copyright. The sale or reuse of the modified design is prohibited. Also, be aware that any modification to plans relieves the original designer from liability for design defects and voids all warranties expressed or implied.

8. WHO IS RESPONSIBLE FOR COPYRIGHT INFRINGEMENT?

Any party who participates in a copyright violation may be responsible including the purchaser, designers, architects, engineers, drafters, homeowners, builders, contractors, sub-contractors, copy shops, blueprinters, developers, and real estate agencies. It does not matter whether or not the individual knows that a violation is being committed. Ignorance of the law is not a valid defense.

9. PLEASE RESPECT HOME DESIGN COPYRIGHTS

In the event of any suspected violation of a copyright, or if there is any uncertainty about the plans purchased, the publisher, architect, designer, or the Council of Publishing Home Designers (www.cphd.org) should be contacted before proceeding. Awards are sometimes offered for information about home design copyright infringement.

10. PENALTIES FOR INFRINGEMENT

Penalties for violating a copyright may be severe. The responsible parties are required to pay actual damages caused by the infringement (which may be substantial), plus any profits made by the infringer commissions to include all profits from the sale of any home built from an infringing design. The copyright law also allows for the recovery of statutory damages, which may be as high as $150,000 for each infringement. Finally, the infringer may be required to pay legal fees which often exceed the damages.

BLUEPRINT PRICE SCHEDULE

PRICE TIERS	1-SET STUDY PACKAGE	5-SET BUILDING PACKAGE	8-SET BUILDING PACKAGE	1-SET REPRODUCIBLE*
A1	$465	$515	$570	$695
A2	$505	$560	$615	$755
A3	$570	$625	$685	$860
A4	$615	$680	$745	$925
C1	$660	$735	$800	$990
C2	$710	$785	$845	$1,055
C3	$775	$835	$900	$1,135
C4	$830	$905	$960	$1,215
L1	$920	$1,020	$1,105	$1,375
L2	$1,000	$1,095	$1,185	$1,500
L3	$1,105	$1,210	$1,310	$1,650
L4	$1,220	$1,335	$1,425	$1,830
SQ1				.40/SQ. FT.
SQ3				.55/SQ. FT.
SQ5				.80/SQ. FT.
SQ7				$1.00 / SQ. FT.
SQ9				$1.25 / SQ. FT.
SQ11				$1.50 / SQ. FT.

PRICES SUBJECT TO CHANGE

* REQUIRES A FAX NUMBER

PLAN #	PRICE TIER	PAGE	SQUARE FOOTAGE	MATERIALS LIST
HPK3100001	L1	4	4299	
HPK3100111	C2	10	1909	
HPK3100002	C2	11	2038	
HPK3100003	C2	12	2071	
HPK3100004	C2	14	2076	
HPK3100005	C2	16	2096	
HPK3100006	C2	18	2125	
HPK3100007	C2	19	2151	
HPK3100008	C2	20	2151	Y
HPK3100009	C2	22	2179	
HPK3100010	C2	24	2215	
HPK3100011	C2	26	2215	
HPK3100012	C2	28	2253	
HPK3100013	C3	30	2256	
HPK3100014	C2	31	2268	
HPK3100015	C2	32	2272	
HPK3100016	C1	34	1942	
HPK3100017	C2	35	2309	

PLAN #	PRICE TIER	PAGE	SQUARE FOOTAGE	MATERIALS LIST
HPK3100018	C2	36	2380	
HPK3100019	C2	38	2394	
HPK3100020	C2	40	2406	
HPK3100021	C2	41	2410	
HPK3100022	C2	42	2410	
HPK3100023	C2	44	2419	
HPK3100024	C2	46	2433	
HPK3100025	C2	48	2438	Y
HPK3100026	C2	50	2441	
HPK3100027	C2	52	2457	
HPK3100028	C2	54	2485	
HPK3100029	C3	55	2545	
HPK3100030	C2	56	2686	
HPK3100031	C2	57	2723	
HPK3100032	C4	58	3102	Y
HPK3100033	C4	63	3062	
HPK3100034	C2	64	2568	Y
HPK3100036	C2	66	2631	Y

ORDER BLUEPRINTS ANYTIME AT EPLANS.COM OR 1-800-521-6797